THE
SALES
COMPENSATION
PLAYBOOK

DESIGNING SALES INCENTIVE PLANS THAT
ALIGN PAY WITH PURPOSE AND PERFORMANCE

BETTINA KAEMMERER

THE SALES COMPENSATION PLAYBOOK

*Designing Sales Incentive Plans That Align Pay
with Purpose and Performance*

ISBN: 978-1-9193066-0-5 (Paperback)
ISBN: 978-1-9193066-1-2 (Hardcover)
ISBN: 978-1-9193066-2-9 (eBook)

First Edition: 2025

CONTENTS

CHAPTER 1

Collaboration & Alignment

The Power of Sales Compensation (cross-group collaboration/ Sales Compensation can't work in isolation)

> **How can organizations ensure that sales compensation drives the right purpose rather than creating misalignment?**

Problem: Sales compensation often works in isolation, misaligning incentives across teams, leading to inefficiencies and lost revenue.

Resolution: A well-structured sales compensation planning approach fosters cross-group collaboration, aligns goals, and becomes a key driver of revenue growth.

What you will read about:

▸ Why sales compensation cannot exist in isolation and the success is depending on cross-group collaboration.
▸ Why sales compensation matters and is one of the most critical levers for business growth.
▸ The psychology of motivation – What makes salespeople tick?
▸ Aligning incentives with business objectives. Focus, Focus, Focus.
▸ Data-driven decision making and transparent communication.

Learnings: After reading this chapter, you will know what is important to structure the sales compensation plan, who to involve and why. You will know how to ensure the sales compensation plan is focusing on the right outcome for your company, the salesperson and the customer.

A well-designed sales compensation plan is the most powerful tool for driving revenue and aligning teams across the business to the company's strategy. When structured effectively, it serves as a bridge between company objectives and frontline execution. However, when done poorly, it can lead to misalignment, inefficiencies, and lost revenue opportunities.

Sales Compensation in Isolation

Too often, sales compensation operates in a silo, disconnected from other business functions. This isolation leads to misaligned plan design Sales compensation can't succeed without collaboration across key departments. Sales compensation need to be interacting with HR, Finance, RevOps / Sales Ops, Marketing, Product Development and of course Leadership. They all play a role in a successful plan design, that is brought together into a tailor-made sales compensation plan by the sales compensation team.

So, what role does everyone play in the project?

Leadership will give you the short and long-term strategy that needs to be translated into a well-balanced sales compensation plan.

HR, which are now often called People & Culture are responsible for remuneration increases, organizational hierarchy changes, lay-offs / restructuring, local labour laws & respective changes to it.

Finance is the team that often owns the budget, either as one number or broken down by country or product or division.

RevOps / SalesOps together with Finance can forecast revenue more accurately because incentive structures are directly tied to desired business outcomes. They can also identify seasonality and managing cost of goods sold (COGS).

Marketing is tasked with generating qualified leads but may go after the wrong ICP (Ideal Customer Profile). By collaborating, they can improve the quality of leads generated. Marketing can also tailor campaigns to support targeted segments or products prioritized in the compensation plan.

Customer Success teams can collaborate with sales on delivering high-value solutions where incentives are aligned. They can also improve the account plan for each prospect / customer.

Product Development will know about products that are retiring, new products and any enhancements that may mean availability for more markets.

When misaligned this creates friction and reduces the overall effectiveness of the go-to-market strategy. The unified focus ensures that the entire company is rowing in the same direction when it comes to driving sustainable revenue growth.

A well-structured sales compensation plan fosters collaboration between departments, aligns goals, and becomes a key driver of revenue growth.

Leadership

Product Development

Finance

SALES COMPENSATION

Customer Success

HR (People & Culture)

Marketing

RevOps / SalesOps

Why Sales Compensation Matters and should be an integral part of your organization

Sales compensation is one of the most critical levers for driving business growth. It does more than simply reward performance—it shapes and directs sales behaviours, ensuring that effort is channelled into the most impactful and strategically aligned activities. The challenge lies in finding the right balance: between performance measures, sales targets, thresholds, tiered pay structures, pay-mix, margins, and profits—all while remaining in harmony with your broader go-to-market strategy and over-arching business objectives. That is a complex task, and it cannot be achieved in isolation. Cross-functional collaboration becomes essential.

A well-structured sales compensation plan encourages revenue growth by financially rewarding high-impact sales activities. It isn't just about rewarding effort; it is about guiding behaviour. Whether it is winning high-value customers, upselling existing accounts, or breaking into new markets, the right plan ensures sales teams are not only working hard, but working smart—with their actions closely aligned to revenue-driving priorities.

Another key benefit of a thoughtfully designed sales compensation plan is its ability to retain top sales talent. High-performing salespeople are often driven by clear, compelling earning potential. When a compensation model transparently links effort to reward and does so in a way that feels both fair and achievable, it becomes a powerful tool for retention. Sales reps who see a tangible, direct path from performance to income are more likely to stay engaged, motivated, and committed to long-term success. The result? Reduced turnover preserved institutional knowledge, and a more stable, high-performing go-to-market engine.

Cross-functional alignment plays a crucial role here. Human Resources and Leadership can collaborate to build a competitive talent strategy that is anchored in both compensation and career development. Operations and enablement teams contribute by equipping sellers with the tools, training, and support they need to hit their goals—and in turn, earn their pay. Culturally, a strong compensation framework reinforces a meritocratic environment where excellence is visible, valued, and rewarded.

Sales compensation also supports long-term business sustainability by aligning short-term incentives with broader strategic goals. One of the most persistent challenges in sales compensation design is the need to balance immediate revenue targets with the long-term vision—whether that is focused on improving customer lifetime value, expanding into new markets, or shifting to a recurring revenue model. When incentives are crafted with these long-term priorities in mind, sales behaviour naturally aligns with the company's future trajectory.

For example, if a business is moving towards a subscription-based model, the compensation plan might place greater emphasis on customer retention and contract renewals. If market expansion is a key initiative, bonuses might reward first-mover wins or vertical-specific penetration. When margin improvement is a strategic focus, incentives could shift to favour high-profit deals over pure top-line revenue.

This kind of alignment ensures that sales teams are not just closing quickly but closing wisely. It is not only about what they achieve, but how they achieve it. For executives and boards, it provides assurance that growth is not just aggressive, but sustainable built on a foundation of intentional planning and smart execution. For departments like Product, Revenue Operations, Marketing, and Finance, it creates confidence in the go-to-market strategy, enabling better coordination and stronger project planning that tie together past lessons, current priorities, and future ambitions.

In essence, sales compensation isn't just a financial mechanism—it is a strategic tool. Done right, it aligns people, performance, and priorities across the entire business.

> **Real-Life Example:** A telecoms provider was struggling with high churn due to salespeople overpromising during sales. By involving Customer Success and Finance in plan design, they added a clawback for early cancellations and bonuses for contract renewals. The result? Customer churn dropped by 18%, and NPS scores improved significantly.

The Psychology of Motivation – What Makes Salespeople Tick?

Sales is a high-pressure, results-driven field where motivation isn't just helpful—it is essential. In an environment where outcomes are everything and performance is constantly measured, understanding what truly drives salespeople is key to unlocking their full potential. And while compensation is the most visible lever, it is far more than just a pay-check. At its core, sales compensation is a behavioural tool—one designed to shape focus, fuel ambition, and sustain momentum.

Monetary rewards remain a central driver. A competitive commission structure, especially when it includes accelerators or uncapped earning potential, taps into the performance-driven mindset of most sales professionals. When earnings scale directly with effort and achievement, motivation naturally intensifies. Salespeople are more likely to push through challenges, chase bigger opportunities, and sustain energy over long sales cycles when there is a clear, compelling financial upside.

But money alone isn't enough. Recognition and status play a powerful psychological role in sales motivation. Leaderboards, president's clubs, achievement badges, and even public shout-outs within teams can ignite a deep sense of pride and competitiveness. These non-monetary rewards satisfy the innate human need for acknowledgment and significance—especially in a role where wins and losses are so visible. Salespeople often thrive on being seen as top performers, and the desire to be recognized can drive consistency, resilience, and extra effort.

Career growth is another critical factor. Sales professionals are ambitious by nature, and many are driven by the promise of progression—whether that is climbing the ranks, leading a team, or moving into strategic roles. Structured incentives that reward skill development, strategic thinking, and leadership behaviour not only improve current performance but also nurture long-term loyalty and professional investment. When sales reps see a path forward—and believe the system will support their advancement—they engage more deeply and stay more committed.

Understanding these psychological levers allows organizations to design sales compensation structures that go beyond simple pay-for-performance. The most effective plans weave together financial incentives, recognition mechanisms, and career-building opportunities into a cohesive motivational ecosystem. When these elements are aligned with company goals and individual aspirations, the result is a sales team that is not only highly productive but genuinely inspired to succeed.

Here are a few examples of monetary and non-monetary rewards:

Pay for Performance: How to make a small pay pot exciting?

Monetary options:

▸ Review very carefully caps, multipliers, kickers, accelerators etc. as you have very little room for mistakes or experiments.

▸ Think Total Compensation! Review also profit sharing, retirement and pension plans, shares or equity, incentives and bonuses, recognition and rewards, holiday and personal time off, professional development programmes, etc.

▸ Your pay needs to be tied to needs, which means you can't be too strict and require more flexibility to ensure fairness. We all are different and have different needs.

▸ Openly communicate why the pay pot is so small and talk up the value.

▸ Go for low-risk plans with more contests to motivate the top sellers and allow the medium or low performers to do an extra stretch. That way you can more easily build in smart caps and keep very tight budget control. Salesforce will be going more into competitive mode to get a bigger portion of the available pot.

Low or non-monetary options:

▸ Granting privileges (e.g. the best salesperson gets to use the CEO office for a day).

▸ Personalized recognition and awards on top of the monetary recognition.

▸ Check with HR in any case if the benefit you are trying to grant, works in all countries (different local laws).

▶ Non-monetary incentives have been used to reward employees for their good work by providing opportunities for training, flexible work schedules, improved work environments and sabbaticals.

Top tip: Get pay right and show the employees how you did it. Your employees will be more satisfied to stay. Hold on tightly to top talent but know when to hold 'em and when to fold 'em. Don't risk losing performers by underpaying them or losing money by overpaying underperformers. Pay extra close attention to flight risks and make careful decisions about which of those risks you can do something about. You may need to increase pay of top employees to retain them and keep your business running smoothly. At the same time, holding low performers at the bottom of their range or even out of range frees up budget to use more wisely. It is really all about making wise choices and keeping a balance.

Even a simple "thank you" can go a long way at times!

Real-Life Example: A cybersecurity firm implemented a tiered bonus plan with monthly recognition badges. One salesperson, previously mid-tier, surged to top performer by aiming for public recognition at sales town halls. Monetary incentives were great—but the public praise drove her consistency.

Aligning Incentives with Business Objectives

In a competitive, fast-moving business environment, focus is everything. Sales compensation plans aren't just about paying your sales teams—they are a critical tool for driving the behaviours that matter most to the business. When thoughtfully designed, incentive plans serve as a direct line between high-level business objectives and day-to-day sales behaviour, creating clarity and alignment across the entire commercial engine.

At the heart of this alignment is the principle that commissions should reward revenue-generating activities that support the company's long-term vision and growth. Whether the goal is to scale rapidly, improve profitability, enter new markets, or drive predictable recurring revenue, the compensation structure must reflect and reinforce those strategic aims. Salespeople should know, without ambiguity, which outcomes matter most—and be financially and emotionally motivated to pursue them.

Striking the right balance when selecting performance measures is critical. Many organizations make the mistake of including too many metrics in their compensation plans, which can dilute focus and confuse priorities. When overwhelmed with multiple objectives, salespeople often gravitate toward the easiest targets—those that are most achievable for them personally—rather than the activities that drive the greatest strategic impact.

To avoid this, it is important to identify and emphasize the one or two key measures that truly matter for each role. For example, Business Development Managers—often referred to as "hunters"—should be incentivized around new logo acquisition, focusing on bringing in fresh customers and expanding the company's reach. In contrast, Account Executives or "farmers" are better suited to targets tied to customer retention, account growth, and long-term relationship management.

By tailoring performance measures to match the core responsibilities of each sales role, and aligning those measures with the broader customer lifecycle, companies create stronger focus and greater impact. This role-specific alignment not only enhances individual performance but also supports more sustainable growth and healthier, more predictable revenue streams.

Of course, no plan can remain static. Markets evolve, customer needs shift, and strategic priorities change over time. That is why compensation effectiveness must be reviewed regularly. By monitoring performance trends, collecting feedback from the field, and analysing how incentives are influencing behaviour, companies can make timely adjustments that keep their plans aligned with real-world dynamics. This kind of agility ensures that the compensation framework remains a source of focus, energy, and strategic alignment—no matter how the landscape changes.

Incentives that are aligned with business goals remove confusion, directed effort in the right way, and make best use of resources. Top-performing teams build sales compensation plans that tie individual success directly to company success.

For example, if the business is prioritizing high-retention, low-churn revenue, but Account Executives are only compensated on closed ARR, you create a misalignment that hurts both growth and retention. A better approach is to tie a portion of variable pay to metrics like net revenue retention (NRR), product adoption in the first 30 days, or qualified customer fit.

Below is a simplified framework showing an example on how roles can align incentives with core business goals:

Role	Business Objective	Aligned Incentive
BDRs (Hunters)	New logo acquisition	Commission per ICP-qualified deal
Account Executives	Drive sustainable ARR growth	Commission on closed ARR with accelerators for multi-year or high-retention deals
AMs (Farmers)	Retention + upsell	Bonuses for expansion + renewals
SDR	Improve pipeline quality	Bonuses for qualified ICP meetings, not volume
Customer Success	Reduce Churn	Incentive for 6-month retention or upsells
Sales Engineer / PreSales	Increase deal velocity	Bonus on technical close support within 30 days

Purpose: Demonstrate how different roles align to different outcomes through incentive structure. These incentives don't just drive behaviour—they act as internal feedback loops. When every team's sales compensation plan supports the company's strategic direction, you eliminate friction and accelerate performance.

Real-Life Example: An edtech company shifting to a subscription model tied bonuses to 12+ month contracts and customer retention. Salespeople, who once focused on quick closes, began qualifying prospects better. Renewals rose 22% in the first two quarters.

Data-Driven Decision Making and Transparent Communication

High-performing sales organizations don't rely on gut feel—they rely on data. But data alone isn't enough. What separates good teams from great ones is the transparency with which that data is shared and used.

Effective compensation begins with a deep understanding of the numbers. Organizations need to analyse available data to ensure that targets are both ambitious and achievable, and that they support healthy margins and sustainable profits. Regularly reviewing performance metrics allows companies to refine their plans over time, making informed adjustments based on what is working and where gaps exist. This kind of data-driven decision making ensures that compensation structures remain aligned with business realities, and that incentives continue to guide the right behaviours.

Equally important is transparency. A great plan is only as effective as its communication. Salespeople need to clearly understand how they are being measured, how they earn their compensation, and what success looks like. When compensation plans are communicated openly—with no hidden terms, vague metrics, or last-minute surprises—it builds trust, drives engagement, and eliminates the confusion that can otherwise erode morale and performance. Those that are supporting the sales teams and maintaining the plan simultaneously need to be kept in the loop and also need to understand what the plan aims for, hence the strategy details, how targets have been set and what the ask is for each team involved in the execution.

Ultimately, the combination of analytical rigor and clear communication transforms compensation from a simple payout system into a strategic, motivational force. It brings clarity, accountability, and alignment across the sales organization—ensuring that every rep knows where to focus and how their efforts contribute to the company's broader success.

When salespeople understand exactly how their pay is calculated, how their performance stacks up, and how company-wide metrics are trending, they trust leadership more and focus on the right actions. That transparency starts with how compensation plans are rolled out and reviewed.

Practical tools to foster clarity:

▸ **Dashboards** showing quota attainment, pipeline coverage, and payout projections
▸ **Monthly 1:1s** to review metrics and reinforce incentives
▸ **Quarterly plan reviews** that explain any adjustments and the reasoning behind them
▸ **Open feedback loops** where sales reps can ask questions and give input on what is working or not

Transparency builds trust, and trust accelerates adoption. A sales compensation plan isn't just a spreadsheet—it is a story you tell your team about what matters.

Case Study: How a SaaS Company Increased Revenue by 30% Challenge

A mid-stage B2B SaaS company was struggling with inconsistent growth. Sales reps were hitting quotas, but new customers churned quickly. The compensation plan rewarded short-term wins, with no penalties or incentives tied to long-term outcomes. Customer Success teams were cleaning up deals that were never a good fit to begin with.

Solution

The RevOps team led a redesign of the entire incentive structure:

▸ **Account Executives** received bonuses only for deals meeting ICP (Ideal Customer Profile) standards
▸ A **clawback clause** was added for customers who churned within 90 days

▸ **Customer Success** compensation included NRR (net recurring revenue) and product activation metrics
▸ **Sales Engineers** were incentivized to shorten sales cycles and improve onboarding accuracy

Implementation

The changes were rolled out over two quarters:

▸ Leadership hosted a transparent sales compensation plan Q&A
▸ Custom dashboards were built to track individual and team performance
▸ Weekly syncs between Sales and CS reinforced cross-functional goals

Results

Within 12 months:

▸ **Revenue grew by 30%**, from $12M to $15.6M ARR
▸ Churn dropped by 40%
▸ Product adoption in the first 60 days improved by 22%

"This was the first time everyone had the same definition of success," said the VP of Revenue Operations. "It changed how we sell, how we support, and how we win."

CONCLUSION

KEY TAKEAWAYS

THE IMPORTANCE OF CROSS-FUNCTIONAL ALIGNMENT

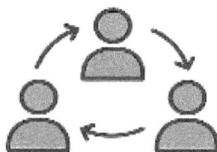

HOW MOTIVATION WORKS IN SALES

TYING COMPENSATION TO COMPANY GOALS

USING DATA AND TRANSPARENCY

WHO TO INVOLVE IN PLANNING

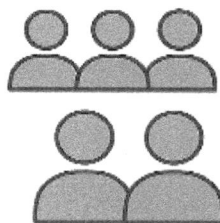

Sales compensation is more than just a pay structure; it is a strategic tool that shapes behaviour, aligns teams, and drives business success. When designed thoughtfully, it fosters collaboration across departments, ensures sales efforts are focused on meaningful outcomes, and becomes a core driver of revenue growth. By integrating cross-group collaboration and focusing on business objectives, organizations can unlock the true power of sales compensation.

CHAPTER 2

Fundamentals & Goal Setting

Sales Compensation Fundamentals (incl. KPI / Goal Setting)

"This chapter is foundational to everything that comes after, so we will be taking more time and pages to ensure that our foundation is solid."

Understanding the basics of sales compensation is essential to setting clear and meaningful goals and structuring pay effectively.

> **What are the key components of an effective sales compensation plan, and how do you set meaningful KPIs?**

Problem: Companies struggle with setting the right pay-mix, quotas, drivers, and KPIs, leading to unmotivated sales teams and missed targets.

Result: Clearly defined compensation structures create a fair, motivating, and performance-driven sales organization.

- The three key components: Base salary, commission and bonuses.
- Pay-Mix: Fixed vs. variable pay – Striking the right balance.
- Quotas, targets and on-target earnings (OTE).
- Sales Cycles: Short / Medium / Long.

Case Study: The impact of applying the right pay-mix by role.

Learnings: After reading this chapter, you will understand the fundamentals of sales compensation and why it is essential to tailor it correctly for each sales role.

A solid understanding of sales compensation fundamentals is the foundation for building an effective, performance-driven sales organization. Without a clear framework in place, even the most ambitious growth targets can fall flat. Too often, companies struggle with getting the core elements right—misaligning pay-mix, setting unrealistic quotas, or choosing KPIs that don't truly reflect success. Even sales organizations that appear perfectly structured can falter when there is confusion around role hierarchy, job titles, responsibilities, and overall team composition. No clear sorting lines or job descriptions. The result? Sales teams become disengaged, motivation declines, and performance suffers.

Without clarity or strategic intent, even the most talented sales professionals will struggle to perform. To avoid this, compensation plans must be built around a clear structure that defines not just how much is paid, but why, when, and for what.

You will be seeing a significant performance shift after aligning pay-mix more closely to role responsibilities. Business development managers receiving a higher variable component tied to new logos and meetings booked, while account managers should be rewarded more for retention and expansion. This clarity not only will drive better individual performance but also improve team collaboration and alignment across the sales funnel.

In the end, getting the fundamentals right isn't just about numbers—it is about creating a structure that motivates, rewards, and drives behaviour in a way that supports the company's broader strategy in a long-term and short-term way. When thoughtfully constructed, sales compensation becomes a powerful tool for growth, engagement, and short-term and long-term success.

The three key components of Sales Compensation: Base Salary, Variable Compensation & Bonuses

Each of these elements plays a distinct role in motivating and retaining a high-performing sales team.

The base salary forms the financial backbone of a sales compensation plan, providing sales professionals with a dependable and steady income. This consistent pay supports job security and allows individuals to manage essential living expenses such as rent or mortgage payments, groceries, and other daily necessities. By meeting these foundational financial needs, base salary reduces stress, promotes stability, and encourages long-term commitment to the organization. Even during periods when sales activity is slow or targets aren't met, team members can rely on this fixed income, which fosters trust, boosts morale, and helps reduce employee turnover.

Variable compensation—commonly known also as sales commission or target incentive—is a performance-based component of the compensation plan that directly ties an individual's earnings to their sales results. Unlike base salary, this portion is not guaranteed; it must be earned through the successful achievement of clearly defined sales goals. These goals should be measurable, meaningful to the business, and realistically attainable through focused effort and consistent performance.

This component is designed to align individual effort with the broader business objectives by providing a clear financial incentive to drive results. It creates a sense of urgency and purpose, encouraging sales professionals to stay engaged, prioritize high-impact activities, and push beyond minimum expectations. Variable compensation plans typically include thresholds for underachievement and overachievement, meaning that earnings can fluctuate based on how well targets are met or exceeded. This structure allows top performers to maximize their income while also signalling when improvement is needed, making it a powerful tool for both motivation and accountability.

Use market data to price each sales role accurately based on both the country in which the employee is located and their level of seniority.

Just like roles in other departments, sales roles should be regularly re-viewed and re-priced to reflect current market conditions. This is im-portant because compensation expectations evolve over time due to factors such as economic shifts, competitive talent landscapes, and changes in industry standards. Failing to keep base salary and sales compensation aligned with the market can lead to difficulties in at-tracting top talent, increased turnover, and potential pay inequities across your organization. Regular benchmarking ensures your com-pensation strategy remains competitive, fair, and effective in motivat-ing performance.

Additionally, the growing emphasis on pay transparency—now a legal requirement in countries like the UK and several others—underscores the need for consistent, data-driven compensation practices. Trans-parent pay structures not only build trust with employees but also sup-port compliance, equity, and fairness. Adopting this approach proac-tively positions your organization as forward-thinking and aligned with emerging global standards.

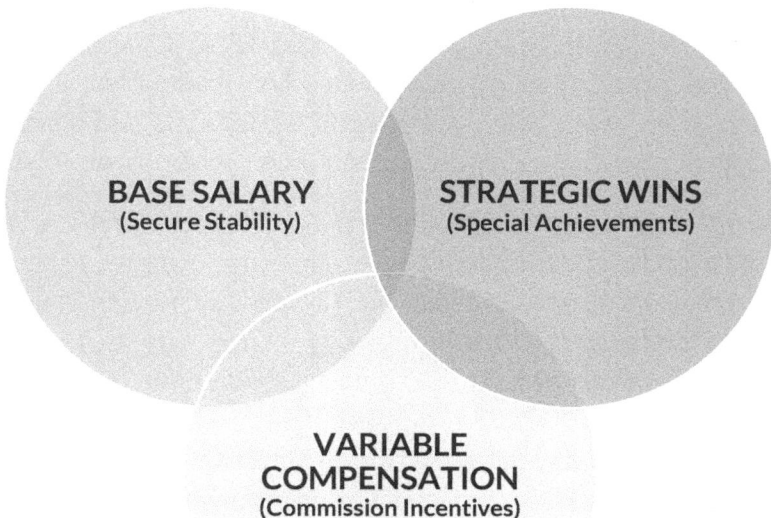

BASE SALARY
(Secure Stability)

STRATEGIC WINS
(Special Achievements)

VARIABLE COMPENSATION
(Commission Incentives)

Real-Life Example: At a SaaS company, Sarah, an Enterprise AE, has a base salary of £60,000 and an OTE of £120,000. She earns 50% of her compensation through variable commission tied to closed deals. When she lands a £200K deal, she gets a £10K bonus on top of her commission due to a strategic focus on enterprise expansion. This layered model rewards both everyday selling and strategic wins. She feels both secure and highly motivated, knowing her income grows with performance.

Pay-Mix: Fixed vs. Variable Pay – Striking the right balance

Striking the right balance between fixed and variable pay is a critical element of an effective sales compensation strategy. When the fixed portion of compensation is too high, it can diminish urgency, reduce motivation to close deals, and make it harder to differentiate top performers. On the other hand, if the variable portion is too aggressive, it can create instability, lead to high stress levels, and even encourage short-term or risky sales behaviours that may harm long-term customer relationships. On-Target Earnings (OTE). For example, a 70/30 pay-mix means 70% of OTE is fixed salary and 30% is variable, performance-based pay.

But what is the *right* mix? That depends on several critical factors: the type of sales role, the sales cycle, the sales representative's influence on buying decisions, and industry benchmarks.

Why the Pay-Mix Balance Matters

When the fixed portion is too high, it may dull motivation and make it hard to distinguish top performers. When the variable portion is too aggressive, it can cause income instability, elevate stress, and even drive risky or short-term selling behaviours that undermine long-term relationships. The right mix motivates the right behaviours—and supports sustainable performance.

To design an effective compensation structure, begin by categorizing sales roles based on selling motions:

Sales Role	Priorities	Compensation Focus
Hunters (e.g., Business Development Reps)	**Focus**: Acquiring new customers, cold outreach, high activity levels **Ideal Pay-Mix**: More aggressive (e.g., 50/50 (mainly US) or 60/40) **Rationale**: Their success is directly measurable and tied to personal effort. Incentives drive performance.	These roles focus on acquiring new business, often through cold outreach and high activity levels. Because success is highly measurable and results are closely tied to individual effort, hunters generally respond well to a compensation model with a higher variable component. This structure rewards aggressive prospecting and deal-closing. If someone talks about 'new logo', they really mean 'new business'.
Farmers (e.g., Account Managers)	**Focus**: Expanding and nurturing existing customer relationships **Ideal Pay-Mix**: Balanced (e.g., 80/20 or 75/25) **Rationale**: Outcomes are often long-term and collaborative; revenue is more predictable.	These roles are more focused on nurturing existing client relationships, driving retention, and generating incremental revenue through upselling or cross-selling. A more balanced mix of fixed and variable pay works well here, as the impact of their work often takes longer to materialize and involves deeper, ongoing collaboration. Their revenue is more predictable and less risky.

Sales Role	Priorities	Compensation Focus
Hybrids (e.g., Territory Managers or Full-Cycle Sellers)	**Focus**: A mix of hunting and farming— both acquisition and retention **Ideal Pay-Mix**: Moderate (e.g., 60/40 or 70/30) **Rationale**: Needs enough fixed pay to support relationship-building, but also incentives for growth.	These roles blend aspects of both hunting and farming. You will find Hybrid roles often, where you do not have enough headcount to have both functions, for example when expanding into new territories or you are a start-up. They may be responsible for acquiring new customers while also maintaining and growing existing accounts. For hybrid roles, a mid-range mix of fixed and variable pay is typically appropriate, offering enough base to support relationship-building while still incentivizing new business development.
Sales Managers	**Focus:** Overseeing teams, coaching, forecasting, and roll-up responsibilities **Ideal Pay-Mix:** Less aggressive (e.g., 80/20) **Rationale:** As their impact is indirect, their mix leans more toward stability with strategic upside.	

By aligning the fixed-variable ratio with the demands of each role, companies can drive the right behaviours, maintain motivation, and build a compensation plan that is both competitive and sustainable.

How to Set the Right Pay-Mix

Benchmark by Industry & Geography: Understand what is standard for your sector and market. Salespeople expect compensation that aligns with regional norms and living standards. **Match Mix to Influence:** The more influence a role has on the purchasing decision, the more aggressive the mix should be. **Ensure Fairness Across Roles:** Align pay-mix within role types and across countries or regions, while allowing flexibility for local market conditions.

There is no one-size-fits-all formula. But by tailoring pay-mix to role requirements, performance drivers, and industry norms, companies can build compensation plans that are motivating, fair, and aligned with business goals.

Real-Life Example: A German MedTech startup had a pay-mix of 80% fixed and 20% variable for its BDRs. The team showed low urgency in booking meetings. After shifting the mix to 60/40 and tying incentives to both meeting volume and lead quality, bookings increased 35% within one quarter. The higher variable pay unlocked competitive drive without harming quality. The lesson? Small tweaks to the mix can drastically change motivation.

Quotas, targets, and on-target earnings (OTE)

Setting meaningful quotas, targets, and on-target earnings (OTE) is a foundational part of a well-designed sales compensation plan. These elements not only define expectations but also serve as key motivators, guiding sales behaviour and aligning individual efforts with broader business goals. There needs to be a ratio between the total target compensation (TTC) of a salesperson and the quota or target in relation to the overall costs.

Quotas are the performance benchmarks that sales professionals are expected to achieve within a defined time frame—most commonly monthly, quarterly, or annually. They serve as a crucial link between individual effort and organizational goals, providing clarity around what success looks like and how it will be measured. When thoughtfully designed, quotas drive performance, focus attention on key objectives, and ensure alignment between the sales team and the broader business strategy.

To be truly effective, quotas must strike a careful balance between being ambitious enough to push for growth and achievable enough to maintain morale and engagement. If quotas are set too low, they will not challenge your salespeople or support meaningful revenue gains. On the other hand, if they are set unrealistically high, they can create frustration, erode trust in leadership, and lead to burnout or turnover. The key is to base quotas on solid, data-informed analysis rather than guesswork or blanket assumptions.

This is where data-driven quota setting comes into play. Effective quotas should take the following into account:

▸ **Historical performance**: What has the salesperson or team achieved in similar past periods?
▸ **Market opportunity**: How much potential demand exists for your product or service in a given region or segment?
▸ **Territory dynamics**: Are there differences in territory size, customer density, competition, or economic conditions that could impact potential performance?

To further enhance the accuracy and fairness of quota setting, it is essential to conduct both whitespace analysis and share-of-wallet analysis:

Whitespace Analysis:

Whitespace Analysis refers to the untapped or underpenetrated market opportunities within a given territory or customer segment. This analysis helps identify where new revenue can realistically come from. It involves examining customer segments, industries, or geographic areas that have not yet been fully explored, allowing quota-setters to understand where there is room to grow. For example, a salesperson might be assigned a territory that includes high-growth industries that have not been approached yet—this would indicate strong whitespace potential and support a higher quota.

Share-of-Wallet Analysis:

Share of wallet looks at how much of a customer's total potential spend in your category is currently going to your business versus competitors. Understanding this metric helps determine upsell and cross-sell opportunities within existing accounts. For instance, if a customer spends $1 million annually on software solutions and your company only captures $250,000 of that, there is a 75% share-of-wallet opportunity remaining. Quotas can be shaped accordingly to push for deeper account penetration, not just new business acquisition.

By integrating whitespace and share-of-wallet analysis into your quota-setting process, you ensure that targets are not only grounded in reality but also strategically aligned with where the greatest potential lies. This makes quotas more equitable, achievable, and motivational leading to higher performance and stronger business outcomes.

Targets, while closely related to quotas, serve a broader strategic function in a sales compensation plan. Whereas quotas typically focus on specific revenue or unit-based performance within a defined period, targets reflect the wider business objectives the company is working toward. These might include increasing overall revenue, driving the adoption of specific products, acquiring new customers, or expanding market presence within key accounts or new geographic regions.

In addition, targets provide essential context for the sales team. When clearly aligned with company strategy, they help salespeople understand not just what they need to achieve, but *why* it matters. This connection to a larger purpose can increase engagement and drive more focused, strategic selling behaviour. For example, if a company's strategic priority is to grow its presence in the healthcare sector, setting a target tied to that goal ensures that sales efforts are concentrated in areas that support long-term growth, even beyond hitting short-term revenue numbers.

SALES COMPENSATION PLAYBOOK \\

If your organization does not formally use targets, it may be beneficial to implement Key Performance Indicators (KPIs) to measure how sales are achieved, not just whether they are achieved. KPIs can track aspects such as customer satisfaction, the rate of returning customers, or deeper penetration within existing accounts. For instance, a salesperson who improves customer satisfaction scores or expands relationships within a major client may be delivering just as much value as one who closes a large deal. These kinds of metrics are particularly useful in roles where long-term relationships, upselling, or service quality are key to sustained success. By focusing on both what gets sold and how it is sold, targets and KPIs together create a well-rounded approach to performance management.

On-target earnings (OTE) resent the total amount of compensation a sales representative can expect to earn when they achieve 100% of their quota. This includes both components of their compensation package: the fixed base salary and the variable performance-based incentive. While it may seem closely related to the previous topics of quotas and targets, OTE belongs in its own category because it acts as a bridge between compensation design and broader financial planning. It is not just about setting goals for sales—it is about ensuring those goals are financially sustainable and aligned with your company's overall business objectives.

A well-calculated OTE directly reflects the value of the sales role within your organization's strategic and financial framework. It helps you balance what you are willing to pay for performance with what you expect in return in terms of revenue, margin, profitability, and growth. For example, if your company aims for a specific revenue growth rate, has targets for EBITDA or profit margins, or relies on certain deal sizes and volumes to hit annual forecasts, those factors must all be accounted for when designing OTE. Overpaying for average performance can erode profitability, while underpaying top performers can lead to high turnover and missed growth opportunities.

This is why developing the right OTE requires you to answer a series of foundational business questions. What revenue growth rate are you targeting this year? What is the average deal size, and how many deals does a typical salesperson need to close annually to meet quota? How much of that revenue can be attributed to the salespersons direct influence? What is the percentage of variable compensation versus base salary that makes sense for your industry and sales model? And finally, how much are you willing to pay out in variable incentives at different levels of performance—say, 80%, 100%, or 120% of quota?

When these inputs are clearly understood, you can model a compensation structure that aligns your OTE with the economics of your business. For example, a salesperson with an OTE of £120,000 whose quota is £1.2 million in annual revenue is effectively costing the company 10% of the revenue they generate—before factoring in profit margins, overhead, and additional costs. This ratio can be compared across roles, teams, or regions to ensure consistency, competitiveness, and alignment with the company's financial goals.

Beyond internal planning, a clearly communicated OTE also provides sales professionals with transparency and motivation. It allows them to see how their efforts convert into earnings and creates a tangible, achievable benchmark for success. When sales understand exactly what they stand to earn—and what it takes to get there—they are more likely to stay focused, engaged, and aligned with your company's growth trajectory.

Together, well-calibrated quotas, aligned targets, and clearly defined OTE give salespeople a roadmap to success—one that is grounded in data, tied to business priorities, and motivating through both financial and professional rewards.

> **Real-Life Example:** An HR tech company set identical £500K annual quotas for all account executives across regions. However, the London AE had a more saturated market, while the Midlands AE had strong whitespace. By adjusting quotas using whitespace and share-of-wallet analysis, performance rose evenly across regions. The London AE's quota dropped to £400K, while the Midlands AE was given £600K. Balanced expectations led to higher motivation and 20% overperformance on both sides.

Sales Cycles: Short / Medium / Long

The length of the sales cycle—whether short, medium, or long—plays a pivotal role in how compensation plans should be structured. Understanding how long it typically takes to close a deal in your business can help you design a plan that not only motivates but also sustains a sales professional's engagement throughout the process.

In **short sales cycles**, where deals are closed within days or weeks, compensation plans often prioritize immediacy and momentum. Salespeople in these roles benefit most from frequent, usually monthly, commission payments tied directly to fast and short-cycle closed deals. Because the sales process is fast paced, with high transaction volume and relatively low complexity, immediate financial rewards can reinforce the behaviours needed to keep deals moving quickly. For example, a salesperson working in retail software or a subscription-based service with a high-volume pipeline may see commissions paid out weekly or monthly to keep energy levels high and the pipeline flowing.

> **Real-Life Example – Short Cycle:** A B2C SaaS company selling monthly subscriptions via inside sales switched to weekly commission payouts. As a result, their salespeople increased daily outreach by 30%. One salesperson closed 12 deals in a week and saw immediate earnings, which reinforced the effort. Attrition dropped sharply in the next quarter.

Medium-length sales cycles, which generally span from several weeks to a few months, require a more sophisticated and strategic approach to compensation. These types of sales are more complex than transactional short-cycle deals, often involving multiple decision-makers, formal evaluation periods, and product demonstrations. In many cases, these deals also include an implementation phase, which adds another layer of complexity and time before the client begins realizing value.

In such sales cycles, commissions are still typically earned upon deal closure. Rather than issuing monthly commission payments, many organizations opt for quarterly payouts, which better align with the extended duration and delivery rhythm of these engagements. This approach helps to smooth compensation over time, reduce administrative churn, and more closely match the revenue recognition patterns within the business.

A successful compensation plan for medium-length sales cycles also requires careful cross-functional coordination. Since these deals frequently involve PreSales engineers, solution architects, contract managers, and legal teams, it is critical to establish a clear process that outlines who is involved and at what stage. Getting these stakeholders involved early—ideally in the discovery or proposal phase—can shorten the sales cycle significantly, reduce last-minute roadblocks, and increase the likelihood of a successful close. Early engagement not only streamlines internal workflows but also builds client confidence in the company's ability to deliver.

To ensure these processes are eatable and scalable, companies should invest in internal alignment and enablement. That includes documenting the sales motion, clarifying approval workflows, and aligning sales incentives with broader operational readiness. The salesperson's success in these situations is not just about closing the deal—it is about orchestrating a coordinated effort that moves the opportunity forward efficiently and responsibly. Compensation should reflect this broader role and support the behaviours that drive complex, consultative sales forward.

> **Real-Life Example – Medium Cycle:** A cybersecurity firm with 2–3-month cycles introduced quarterly bonuses tied to both signed deals and successful handoffs to implementation. One AE partnered early with a solutions engineer to accelerate a $75K deal by 3 weeks. Their aligned bonus was paid out that quarter, incentivizing repeated collaboration.

In contrast, **long sales cycles**—which may span six months, a year, or even longer—pose even greater challenges for compensation planning. These deals typically involve high-value, complex solutions, often customized or tailored to specific client needs. They require long design and proposal phases, stakeholder alignment across multiple departments, and detailed implementation or rollout plans. Salespeople working on long-cycle deals must be highly skilled in relationship-building and must remain focused over extended periods without the immediate gratification of frequent deal closures.

In these cases, traditional commission structures based solely on deal closure can be demotivating, especially if it may take a year or more before a salesperson sees a payout. To keep motivation high and performance steady, companies often introduce more adaptive compensation mechanisms. One such tool is a recoverable draw, where a salesperson receives regular payments in advance of commission earnings. These recoverable draws are reconciled against future commissions and may be subject to clawback provisions if the deal falls through or the salesperson leaves before completion. This approach ensures financial stability while also protecting the company from overpayment on unclosed business.

Another strategy involves the use of milestone-based bonuses, which reward the salesperson for achieving key progress points throughout the sales journey. These could include successfully completing a proof of concept, securing a signed letter of intent, or obtaining executive buy-in. These bonuses recognize the value of sustained effort and allow salespeople to earn along the way—without needing to wait for the final signature.

Additionally, retention-based incentives can be tied to the long-term success of the client relationship. For instance, a final bonus might only be paid once the client has been live with the product for a specified period or has completed an implementation with a satisfactory outcome. This ensures alignment between sales and delivery teams and incentivizes salespeople to prioritize the right deals—not just the fastest-closing ones.

Together, these more advanced compensation strategies help manage the inherent complexity and extended timeframes of medium and long sales cycles. By designing incentive structures that reflect the realities of the sales process, companies can keep their teams motivated, improve forecasting accuracy, and ensure that compensation is aligned with value creation for the business.

Real-Life Example – Long-Cycle: An enterprise software vendor adopted milestone bonuses for deals exceeding $1M with 9–12-months cycles. One sales representative secured internal stakeholder sign-off after 5 months, triggering a 20% milestone bonus. They later earned a final payout after client onboarding was complete 6 months post-close—totalling $90K in variable pay across 15 months.

	Short-Cycle	Medium-Cycle	Long-Cycle
Pro	High motivation; easy to understand	Encourages consistent performance; rewards overperformance	Rewards retention; builds loyalty; Strong long-term alignment; Drives long-term customer commitment
Con	Income volatility; risk of short-term thinking May reward activity over results	Requires good quota setting Lulls possible early in quarter	Delayed gratification; can plateau; Value depends on company success
Best For	High-volume, short-cycle sales (retail, insurance, door-to-door)	Complex sales, tech sales, Account management, renewals	Subscription services, insurance; Strategic enterprise accounts

	Short-Cycle	Medium-Cycle	Long-Cycle
Sales Type	B2C sales, inside sales	Channel sales, Enterprise SaaS	B2B with long contract terms
	New sales teams or pipeline building		

It is not very motivating to see a payslip that has no sales commission payment in it. Hence the need to adjust pay-out frequency to the sales cycle is important, because less de-motivating.

The goal in all scenarios is to match the pace and structure of the sales process with financial incentives that maintain engagement without causing burnout or disillusionment. If incentives come too late in a long cycle, a salesperson may lose motivation or shift focus. If they are too frequent in a long, complex sale, the company may end up rewarding effort over actual outcomes. Designing compensation to match sales cycle length ensures that performance is recognized appropriately and that the sales force stays focused, resilient, and aligned with the company's long-term revenue goals.

Case Study: The impact of applying the right pay-mix by role

A fast-growing technology company facing scaling challenges recognized that its one-size-fits-all approach to sales compensation was limiting the performance of its revenue-generating teams. The company had been applying a uniform pay structure across all sales roles—offering a similar mix of base salary and variable compensation regardless of each role's specific responsibilities or influence on revenue. This led to several issues: Business Development Managers (BDMs) lacked the urgency to aggressively fill the pipeline, while Customer Success Managers (CSMs) were unclear on how their compensation tied to long-term account growth or customer retention. The result was inconsistent performance, limited cross-functional collaboration, and difficulty forecasting revenue.

To address this, the company undertook a full review of its go-to-market strategy and compensation framework. Working closely with HR, sales leadership and finance, they segmented the revenue team by function and recalibrated the pay-mix to reflect the core value each role brought to the customer journey.

For BDMs, who were primarily responsible for top-of-funnel activities such as booking qualified meetings and generating pipeline, the company increased the proportion of variable compensation in their pay-mix. The new structure placed heavier emphasis on individual activity-based metrics like meetings scheduled with ideal customer profiles, and the value of pipeline generated that successfully moved to later stages. This shift encouraged BDMs to be more targeted, persistent, and strategic in their outreach—aligning compensation with the behaviours that contributed directly to sales team success.

Meanwhile, CSMs were evaluated and incentivized on a completely different set of outcomes. Rather than focusing on short-term activity, their new compensation plan centred around net revenue retention and renewal rates—metrics that reflected their role in maintaining and expanding customer relationships. The variable component of their pay was restructured to reward longer-term client satisfaction, contract renewals, and upsell performance. The company also implemented milestone incentives tied to onboarding success, product adoption, and customer health scores, encouraging proactive engagement and a consultative approach throughout the customer lifecycle.

The results were significant. Within six months of implementing the revised compensation structures, performance metrics improved across both teams. BDMs consistently exceeded their meeting quotas and contributed more qualified leads to the sales funnel. CSMs, in turn, reduced churn, improved upsell conversion, and created more stable recurring revenue streams. The clearer differentiation in pay-mix between roles not only sharpened individual focus but also strengthened collaboration between teams. Sales and customer success began working together more fluidly, with each team understanding how their goals were interconnected and supported by the compensation model.

Perhaps most importantly, the company saw a stabilization in revenue consistency—fewer surprises in pipeline performance and greater predictability in renewals and expansion. By aligning compensation with role-specific responsibilities and outcomes, the company created a more performance-oriented, cross-functional culture that supported sustainable growth.

This case underscores how critical it is to tailor pay structures to the actual impact and time horizon of each role. A well-aligned pay-mix not only motivates individuals in the right way but also creates organizational clarity, encourages teamwork, and leads to more consistent revenue outcomes.

Real-Life Example – Pay-Mix Case: A cloud infrastructure start-up in Texas restructured its compensation plans after noticing stagnant CSM growth. By shifting 30% of CSM bonuses to NRR (Net Revenue Retention), expansion revenue grew 22% YoY. BDRs, incentivized on pipeline quality instead of lead volume, doubled SQL rates. Both teams reported higher morale and alignment.

CONCLUSION

Understanding the fundamentals of sales compensation is critical to building a plan that motivates performance, drives business results, and aligns individual goals with company strategy. A well-designed compensation structure does more than distribute pay—it actively influences behaviour, reinforces priorities, and keeps the sales team aligned with strategic goals. It ensures that individuals understand not only what they are working toward, but also how their success contributes to the organization's growth.

When compensation is thoughtfully structured around clear roles, measurable outcomes, and aligned incentives, it becomes a powerful tool for shaping a high-performing sales culture. The right plan rewards the outcomes that matter, keeps momentum strong, and helps build a motivated, focused team. Getting these basics right isn't just a tactical exercise—it is a strategic move that sets the foundation for long-term success.

Getting the fundamentals right is the first step to creating a sales compensation plan that not only works—but wins. By building a strong foundation based on role clarity, measurable KPIs, and strategic alignment, companies set the stage for sustainable growth and high-performance culture.

The foundation of a winning compensation plan is built on:

- ▶ Role-specific design
- ▶ Sales cycle-aligned timing
- ▶ Metrics that matter
- ▶ Strategic alignment with growth objectives

Getting the fundamentals right is not just operational—it is strategic. Done right, sales compensation becomes a growth engine for the business.

CHAPTER 3

Strategy & Principles

Aligning Sales Compensation with Business Strategy - Principles

Sales Compensation must evolve in-line with company strategy to sustain growth.

> **How should sales compensation be structured to align with overall business strategy and objectives to get to a purposeful sales plan?**

Problem: Sales compensation plans often reward behaviours that don't align with the company's business strategies, often prioritizing quick wins over sustainable growth.

Result: A well-aligned plan drives the right behaviours, balancing new customer acquisition, retention, growth and profitability over just getting the 'low hanging fruit'.

- ▸ How sales compensation plans differ in start-ups vs. enterprises. Impact of company size.
- ▸ Incentivising new customer acquisition vs. retention.
- ▸ How different business models (SaaS, hardware, services) require different incentives.
- ▸ Adapting sales compensation as the company grows and evolves.
- ▸ Top 3 Sales Compensation Mistakes to Avoid.

Real-World Example: Why Salesforce structures sales compensation differently across product lines.

Learnings: This chapter guides you in shaping sales compensation plans that actively support strategic business goals. You will be equipped to design incentive structures that promote long-term value creation—balancing acquisition, retention, and profitability—tailored to company stage, size, and business model.

For a sales compensation plan to deliver meaningful results, it must be closely aligned with the company's evolving business strategy. Sales compensation should not just reward activity—it should reinforce purpose. The value of a strong compensation plan lies in how it shapes sales behaviour to support long-term growth, customer value, and strategic goals. When thoughtfully designed, such a plan serves both as a motivational engine and a strategic instrument, ensuring that every sales interaction contributes to the broader organizational goals.

A common and costly mistake in sales compensation is failing to align incentives with the right objectives. Too often, plans are structured to reward short-term achievements—such as high volumes or quickly closed deals—without considering their long-term impact. This can lead to a misalignment where sales teams prioritize immediate gains over enduring customer relationships, retention, or profitability. In such cases, compensation inadvertently drives counterproductive behaviours, undermining the strategic intent of the business. Therefore, it is essential not only to reward *what* is achieved, but also *how* it is achieved. To be clear: Incentives should reflect not just what is sold, but how it is sold—rewarding ethical, customer-centric, and value-driven behaviours.

The approach and integrity with which deals are closed—focusing on customer needs, solution fit, and long-term value—are critical indicators of sustainable success. When salespeople are incentivized to win business the right way, with both short-term goals and long-term relationships in mind, the organization is far more likely to achieve lasting growth and strategic alignment.

Conversely, a well-aligned compensation plan fosters purposeful selling by guiding salespeople to balance their efforts across acquiring new customers, nurturing existing relationships, expanding accounts, and driving profit. Rather than encouraging a focus on short-lived victories or superficial metrics, it promotes a disciplined, value-oriented approach to selling. This strategic alignment not only enhances sales effectiveness but also creates a more engaged, consistent, and strategically impactful sales force—one that plays a central role in advancing the company's mission and achieving long-term success.

Key Principle: Don't just pay for activity. Pay for strategic outcomes achieved the right way.

Start-ups vs. Enterprises: How Company Size and Stage Impact Sales Compensation

So... how do you tailor compensation for different types of organizations?

Sales compensation strategies are deeply influenced by a company's size, type, structure, and stage of growth. A one-size-fits-all approach rarely works, as the priorities and challenges of a start-up differ significantly from those of a mature enterprise.

Aligning Sales Compensation with Company Stage

START-UP	GROWTH	ENTERPRISE
• Speed	• Scale	• Margin
• New logos	• Retention	• Loyalty
• Awareness	• Unit economics	• Cross-sell
Simple, aggressive, top-line driven	Role-specific, balanced acquisition + expansion	Complex, multi-metric, collaborative incentives

In early-stage start-ups, the primary focus is typically on speed, market penetration, and building an initial customer base. As a result, compensation plans often emphasize aggressive incentives for new customer acquisition. Simplicity is key—commissions tend to be straightforward and heavily weighted toward top-line revenue generation, encouraging rapid sales cycles and a high volume of activity. Flexibility is also essential at this stage, as sales roles may be less defined and team members often wear multiple hats.

As companies scale into growth-stage businesses, their compensation models usually evolve to reflect shifting priorities. While new business remains important, greater emphasis is placed on developing scalable processes, increasing customer retention, and improving unit economics. At this stage, compensation plans may begin to differentiate by role—such as hunters vs. farmers or inside sales vs. field reps—and include more structured metrics tied to customer success, renewals, and expansion revenue.

In large, established enterprises, the sales compensation strategy becomes more sophisticated and multi-dimensional. With mature customer bases and well-defined go-to-market functions, the focus often shifts toward account growth, long-term relationships, cross-sell opportunities, and profitability. Compensation plans in these environments tend to be highly nuanced, involving multiple performance metrics, role-based incentives, and alignment with cross-functional objectives. There may also be a greater emphasis on governance, compliance, and performance management to ensure consistency across global or regional teams.

Ultimately, understanding where a company is in its lifecycle is essential for designing a sales compensation plan that supports both current priorities and long-term strategic goals. Tailoring incentives to match the evolving needs of the business ensures that sales efforts remain aligned, effective, and scalable.

Stage	Priorities	Compensation Focus
Startup	Speed, new logos, awareness	Simple, aggressive, top line driven
Growth	Scale, retention, unit economics	Role-specific, mix of acquisition + expansion
Enterprise	Margin, loyalty, cross-sell	Complex, multi-metric, collaborative incentives

In a well-structured sales organization, not all sales roles serve the same purpose—and their incentives should not either. Different phases of the customer journey demand different behaviours, and sales compensation should be tailored accordingly to reinforce those behaviours. For instance, sales representatives focused on new business acquisition are typically tasked with generating leads, closing first-time deals, and bringing in new customers, also called new logo. To instil urgency and maintain a competitive edge, new business roles are often held to strict performance expectations, including minimum thresholds that must be met to qualify for sales commissions. At the same time, these roles are typically rewarded with accelerators for surpassing their targets, offering higher payout rates once quotas are exceeded. This structure is designed to recognize and reinforce the hustle, persistence, and proactive effort required to win new business and fuel growth.

However, the work doesn't end once a deal is signed. As customers move beyond the acquisition phase, maintaining and expanding those relationships becomes critical to long-term profitability. This is where account managers and customer success teams come into play. Their roles are centred on deepening engagement, ensuring satisfaction, and identifying opportunities for upselling or cross-selling. Compensation for these roles should be aligned with outcomes like customer retention, contract renewals, expansion revenue, and Net Promoter Score (NPS). Long-term incentives tied to recurring revenue or multi-year growth can also help promote a focus on value creation rather than short-term gain.

Aligning incentives with each stage of the customer lifecycle ensures that every team member—whether bringing in new clients or nurturing existing ones—is motivated to act in ways that are both strategically aligned and sustainable. This kind of role-specific alignment creates a more coordinated and effective sales ecosystem, one where every touchpoint with the customer contributes to lasting business success.

Business Models Require Tailored Plans

The structure of a company's business model has a profound impact on how its sales compensation plan should be designed. Different revenue models, cost structures, and sales cycles call for distinct incentives that align with what drives value in each type of business. A one-size-fits-all approach simply doesn't work—each model requires its own unique set of performance metrics and motivational levers.

SaaS companies typically rely on recurring revenue streams, which makes customer retention, renewals, and account expansion critical to long-term success. Compensation plans in this space often include incentives tied to annual contract value (ACV), net revenue retention (NRR), and minimizing customer churn. Salespeople may also be rewarded for securing multi-year deals or upselling new modules or features to existing customers.

Fast-Moving Consumer Goods (FMCG) companies operate in high-volume, low-margin environments where scale, speed, and distribution efficiency are key to profitability. Sales compensation in this sector often focuses on hitting volume targets, driving market share, and ensuring product availability across retail channels. Incentives may be tied to shelf placement, promotional execution, territory coverage, or growth within specific product categories. Because success often depends on relationships with distributors, wholesalers, and retail partners, some roles may also be rewarded based on the effectiveness of channel management and the ability to launch and support new products quickly. Timeliness, execution, and consistency are critical, making performance metrics highly operational in nature.

Hardware companies tend to operate on more transactional models, emphasizing deal volume and upfront margins. Incentive plans here often include SPIFs (Sales Performance Incentive Funds), bonuses, or tiered commissions based on the number of units sold, deal size, or speed of close. Because margins can fluctuate based on product mix, compensation may also include profitability thresholds to maintain discipline around pricing.

Services-based businesses focus heavily on customer relationships and long-term engagement. In these models, salespeople might be compensated based on the length or scope of contracts signed, cross-sell success into adjacent service lines, or utilization rates of billable resources. Incentives may also be linked to customer satisfaction or ongoing client engagement metrics, especially where delivery teams play a key role in revenue realization.

Retailers often have high transaction volumes and relatively low margins, which shifts compensation priorities toward driving foot traffic, increasing basket size, or meeting store-level targets. In some retail environments, bonuses may be tied to daily or weekly sales performance, customer conversion rates, or upselling complementary products at point-of-sale.

Manufacturers frequently have long sales cycles and complex distribution channels, sometimes involving resellers, distributors, or OEM (Original Equipment Manufacturer) partnerships. Compensation in this context may be based on volume commitments, new channel acquisition, or geographic expansion. For direct sales roles, incentives might include bonuses for penetrating new markets, managing key accounts, or securing strategic contracts.

Tailoring compensation to the business model ensures that sales behaviour aligns with the economic drivers of the company. By tying incentives to the metrics that truly matter for each type of organization, businesses can create plans that are not only fair and motivating but also strategically effective.

Tailoring to Business Models

- ▸ **SaaS**: ACV, NRR, churn, upsells
- ▸ **Hardware**: Deal size, SPIFs (Sales Performance Incentive Funds), gross margin thresholds
- ▸ **FMCG**: Volume, execution, channel coverage
- ▸ **Professional Services**: Contract scope, utilization, client retention
- ▸ **Retail**: Daily performance, upsell rate, basket size
- ▸ **Manufacturing**: Channel growth, volume commitments, strategic wins

Business Models Require Tailored Plans

SaaS	Hardware	FMCG	Professional Services	Retail	Manufacturing
ACV, NRR, churn, upsells	Deal size, SPIFs gross margin thresholds	Volume execution channel coverage	Contract scope utilization, client retention	Daily performance upsell rate basket size	Channel growth, volume commitments strategic wins

Sector-Specific Examples

SaaS – Recurring Revenue Focus

Example: HubSpot redesigned its AE compensation plans to focus on *Net Revenue Retention* and multi-year deals, not just new logos. This shift boosted upsell rates and improved churn by 17% within a year.

Hardware – Deal Size & Margins

Example: Cisco pays reps based on deal profitability, not just volume, using margin-based thresholds. This improved price discipline and shifted sales behaviour toward value-selling, especially in competitive bids.

FMCG – Volume, Execution, Reach

Example: Unilever uses compensation tied to *perfect store execution*, territory coverage, and on-shelf availability. Field reps are incentivized on monthly product visibility KPIs, ensuring tight alignment with brand goals.

Professional Services – Relationship & Scope

Example: Accenture compensates client partners on multi-year contract value, client satisfaction, and upsell into adjacent services. This encourages long-term thinking and deeper customer relationships.

Retail – Speed & Conversion

Example: Apple Store staff are not commissioned on individual product sales. Instead, team bonuses are tied to *overall store performance*, NPS, and solution-based bundling—supporting customer trust over hard selling.

Manufacturing – Channel & Territory Growth

Example: Caterpillar rewards sales representatives on *new dealer onboarding*, regional sales growth, and strategic account penetration. This supports long-cycle deals and builds channel strength in emerging markets.

Adapting Sales Compensation Over Time - Why it must evolve alongside strategy, growth stage, and market shifts.

Sales compensation is not a "set-it-and-forget-it" mechanism—it must evolve in tandem with the company's strategic direction, growth stage, and market conditions. As businesses expand, shift focus, or introduce new products, compensation plans should be revisited and adjusted to ensure they continue to drive the right behaviours. For example, a company transitioning from a growth-at-all-costs phase to a profitability-focused model may need to shift incentives away from top-line revenue toward metrics like gross margin, customer lifetime value, or multi-year deal structures.

Compensation plans are not "set and forget."

Revise annually—or whenever your GTM strategy changes.

Ideally, sales compensation is treated as a dynamic, evolving element of a company's go-to-market strategy—not a static tool. As a business grows, pivots, or matures, the assumptions and objectives that once guided its sales incentive structure may become outdated or even counterproductive. What works well for a company in early stage hypergrowth may fall short in a more mature phase that emphasizes operational efficiency, profitability, and customer lifetime value.

For instance, in the early days of a company, particularly in high-growth environments like technology start-ups, the primary goal may be market share acquisition. Sales compensation plans in this context often lean heavily on aggressive new customer acquisition targets, with high variable pay tied to top-line revenue. This structure helps drive rapid momentum and brand visibility. However, as the company matures and stabilizes its market position, the focus often shifts toward customer retention, increasing wallet share, and improving overall unit economics. Continuing to reward sales reps solely for new logos in such a phase can lead to an overemphasis on acquisition, neglecting the valuable, long-term revenue streams that come from expanding and retaining existing accounts.

Furthermore, as companies scale, the sales organization itself often becomes more complex. New roles emerge, including customer success managers, renewal specialists, solution engineers, and partner managers. Each of these roles plays a different part in delivering customer value and driving revenue—and each requires a distinct incentive structure that reflects their specific responsibilities. Compensation plans must also begin to incorporate more sophisticated performance metrics that account not just for deal volume, but for profitability, deal quality, strategic alignment, and even collaborative behaviours across departments. Cross-functional alignment—across product, marketing,

SALES COMPENSATION PLAYBOOK

finance, and customer success—is crucial to ensure compensation plans reinforce shared goals and reduce friction.

In addition to internal changes, external market forces—such as competitive pressure, regulatory shifts, or technological disruption—may require companies to adjust their compensation strategies to stay aligned with new realities. Failing to evolve the sales incentive model alongside the business can result in misaligned behaviours, missed opportunities, and internal friction.

Ultimately, regularly reviewing and adapting sales compensation plans ensures that they remain relevant and strategically aligned. It allows the organization to reward the behaviours that matter most at each stage of growth—whether that is landing flagship clients, deepening existing relationships, improving retention, or increasing margins. A purposeful, responsive compensation strategy supports not only short-term performance but also long-term, sustainable success.

Adapting as You Grow

- ▶ Early-stage = Speed.
- ▶ Scale-up = Process and retention.
- ▶ Later-stage = Margins and stability.

Top 3 Sales Compensation Mistakes to Avoid

1. Overemphasizing short-term wins at the expense of long-term value
2. Using the same plan across all roles, products, or stages
3. Failing to review and adapt plans as strategy evolves

Ultimately, the most effective sales compensation plans are not static—they adapt alongside the company's goals, market position, and strategic priorities. When sales incentives are in sync with business strategy, the result is more than just improved performance; it is a purpose-driven, high-impact sales organization capable of scaling sustainably and delivering real, measurable value over time.

Key Takeaways:

▶ Sales compensation is a strategic tool, not a standalone lever
▶ Align incentives with company stage, strategy, and roles
▶ Tailor plans for business models (SaaS, hardware, services, etc.)
▶ Continuously evolve plans as strategy shifts
▶ Avoid misalignments that encourage unproductive behaviours
▶ Real-world examples show how compensation can drive growth, retention, and focus

Real-Life Example: Salesforce's Compensation Strategy

Salesforce, a global leader in cloud-based customer relationship management (CRM) software, offers a compelling example of how compensation can be strategically aligned with business goals. As a company with a broad and evolving product portfolio, Salesforce recognizes that a uniform incentive structure would not effectively drive the behaviours needed across its diverse sales teams. Instead, the company employs a differentiated compensation strategy tailored to the maturity and strategic importance of each product line.

For teams focused on Salesforce's core, mature offerings—such as its flagship Sales Cloud and Service Cloud—the compensation plans are designed to prioritize customer retention, contract renewals, and account expansion. These teams are typically measured on metrics like net revenue retention, customer satisfaction, and upsell success, reflecting the need to sustain and grow value within established accounts.

In contrast, sales teams working on newer or strategically emerging products, such as AI-driven analytics tools or industry-specific solutions, are incentivized to drive market penetration and capture early wins. Their compensation plans often emphasize net-new customer acquisition, first-year contract value, and strategic account conversions, encouraging a more entrepreneurial approach aimed at building market presence and validating new solutions.

By aligning incentives to the distinct goals of each product group, Salesforce ensures that its go-to-market strategy is supported at every level. This approach allows the company to optimize for both growth and stability—motivating sales teams to drive innovation in emerging areas while maintaining strong performance in its established business lines. It is a dynamic, role-specific model that demonstrates the power of compensation as a lever for strategic execution.

Salesforce doesn't use one compensation plan. It adapts incentives by **product line maturity**:

- **Mature Products (e.g., Sales Cloud)**: Compensation plans drive *retention, upsell, expansion.*
- **Emerging Products (e.g., AI & Industry Clouds)**: Compensation plans push *market entry, new logos, early adoption.*

This ensures the right go-to-market behaviours are reinforced—driving stability where needed and innovation where it matters most.

Real-Life Example: Strategy-Aligned Sales Compensation in Practice

A mid-sized European SaaS provider shifted its sales compensation plans when pivoting from hypergrowth to profitability.

- **Old Model:** SDRs paid on meetings booked; AEs on top-line revenue.
- **New Model:** SDRs comped on SQL-to-pipeline conversion. AEs on gross margin + multi-year contracts.

Result: Churn dropped by 19%, average deal size grew 28%, and pipeline forecasting accuracy improved.

——— CONCLUSION ———

Sales compensation isn't just about payouts—it is a strategic lever that shapes behaviour and drives sustainable growth. When thoughtfully designed and continuously refined, a compensation plan becomes a unifying force that ensures every sales effort reinforces the company's broader goals.

Throughout a company's lifecycle—from the fast-paced early days of a start-up to the complex demands of a global enterprise—the structure of sales incentives must evolve. Start-ups may prioritize speed and market entry, while mature organizations emphasize retention, profitability, and role specialization. Each stage, and each business model—whether SaaS, hardware, services, retail, manufacturing, or FMCG—demands a unique approach to incentives that reflects what truly creates value.

Equally important is aligning compensation with different roles and phases of the customer journey. New business sales representatives thrive on upfront rewards for acquisition, while account managers and customer success teams should be incentivized around long-term outcomes like expansion, retention, and satisfaction. Real-world examples, such as Salesforce, demonstrate how companies can strategically differentiate plans across product lines to match specific growth objectives.

The most common pitfall is misalignment—rewarding behaviours that contradict long-term strategy. Plans that focus too heavily on short-term wins or low-hanging fruit risk undermining profitability, retention, and customer value. To avoid this, compensation structures must consider not just *what* is being sold, but *how* it is being sold, and *why* it matters in the broader context of the business.

CHAPTER 4

Plan Design & Elements

*Designing a Sales Compensation Plan That Works
(drive the right behaviour) - Elements*

A well-structured sales compensation plan is more than a payout mechanism—it is a strategic tool that aligns sales activities with company priorities and delivers sustained value to the business, the salesperson, and the customer. When executed properly, it creates a win-win-win outcome for all stakeholders.

> **How do different sales compensation models compare, and how can you select the most effective one?**

Problem: Many sales compensation plans are overly complex, unclear, or encourage the wrong behaviours.

Result: A clear, structured, and well-aligned plan ensures sales reps stay focused on the right activities while feeling fairly compensated.

Aspects of a plan / The 11-step framework for designing a compensation plan:

1. Eligibility: Defining sales roles and responsibilities. (Hunters / Farmers / Hybrid)
2. Drivers: Setting measurable objectives.
3. Payment: Determining pay-mix (base vs. variable).
4. Trends: Subscription-based sales and multi-year contracts.
5. Payout frequency: Pay close to the selling event.

6. Target setting: Structuring quotas, uplifts, roll-ups.
7. Communicating and rolling out the plan.
8. Governance and compliance.
9. Plan evaluation and iteration.
10. Tools, systems & automation.
11. Behavioural economics & motivation psychology.

Case Study: Successful Sales Compensation Plan rollouts.

Learnings: This chapter equips you to build a sales compensation plan that is practical, motivating, and aligned with business priorities. You will be able to apply a clear framework to create plans that drive the right behaviours, support team performance, and evolve with changing sales strategies—ensuring sustainable success for all stakeholders.

While we have touched on the fact that a well-designed sales compensation plan is more than just a mechanism for paying salespeople, it is worth emphasizing just how strategic this tool truly is. When thoughtfully developed, a sales compensation plan serves as a powerful lever that aligns with company goals leading toward both achieving the immediate targets and long-term aspirations. It not only incentivizes the right behaviours but also aligns individual performance with team and organizational goals, reinforcing the company's core priorities. In doing so, it creates a sustainable foundation for success—one where the business grows, salespeople are energized and fairly rewarded, and customers experience greater value through more focused and consistent service. This kind of plan doesn't just support a sales culture—it helps define and elevate it.

However, the full potential of a sales compensation plan is only realized when all critical elements are considered in its design. Too often, plans fall short because they are created in isolation, disconnected from broader business strategies or the operational realities of the sales organization. Key components—such as role-specific metrics, quota-setting logic, territory fairness, accelerators, thresholds, organizational set-up, pay-mix and clear communication mechanisms—are overlooked or underestimated. Seemingly minor design choices can have disproportionate effects—

causing confusion, misaligned incentives, or a sense of unfairness that erodes trust and motivation. When these vital elements are neglected, plans can become overly complex, lack transparency, or even encourage the wrong behaviours. Sales reps may chase metrics that aren't aligned with meaningful outcomes or struggle to understand how their performance translates into compensation. In many organizations, legacy compensation structures or individually negotiated packages persist without strategic oversight. As a result, similar roles—such as hunters across different markets—may receive unequal pay-mix structures despite performing comparable work. While total compensation should reflect market-specific benchmarks, the underlying pay principles (e.g., pay-mix ratios, incentive logic) should be standardized to ensure fairness and consistency. Total compensation should align with local market benchmarks, pay structure and mix should remain consistent across similar roles globally to ensure fairness. Surely, they will have a different total target compensation, as aligned to the market data, but bands, pay-mix should be equal. This often results in missed targets, team frustration, and demotivation.

In contrast, when all components of a sales compensation plan are deliberately and cohesively integrated—from the strategic intent down to the day-to-day mechanics—the plan becomes a source of clarity and motivation. It acts as a steady guidepost for sales professionals, making expectations transparent and attainable, and reinforcing consistency and fairness across the team. Salespeople know exactly what they're working toward, how they will be measured, and how their success supports both their own goals and the company's broader mission. In this way, a well-rounded and well-executed compensation plan becomes more than a pay model—it becomes a catalyst for performance, alignment, and long-term business success.

The 11-Step Framework for Designing an Effective Sales Compensation Plan

Designing a sales compensation plan that truly drives performance and supports strategic goals requires more than just setting commission rates or assign quotas. It demands a structured approach that considers the diverse dynamics of each and every sales role, all business models, and organizational priorities. The following seven foundational elements serve as a comprehensive framework for building a compensation plan that is not only effective but also scalable, fair, and motivating.

1. Eligibility

The first step is to define precisely which roles within the organization are eligible for variable compensation. Not every sales-related position should be included by default. Roles should be assessed based on their influence over the buying decision and revenue outcomes. This includes distinguishing between hunters, who focus on acquiring new business; farmers, who manage and grow existing accounts; and hybrid roles that span both functions. Customizing compensation plans by role ensures that incentives are relevant to each salesperson's responsibilities and avoids a one-size-fits-all approach that can lead to misaligned behaviour or disengagement. Base your eligibility criteria on impact on negotiating and closing a deal and the measurability of such. It could look like this:

Customer Interaction Frequency: The salespersons role involves regularly engaging with both potential and existing customers, building strong relationships through direct and personal interaction.

Persuasive Selling: The salesperson consistently take an active, hands-on approach in persuading key decision-makers to invest in the company's products, services, or solutions.

Impact Measurement: The salesperson is held accountable to specific, measurable sales targets or quotas that can be directly influenced within each fiscal year.

Tracking & Attribution: The sales efforts are closely tracked, ensuring the salesperson receives accurate credit for customer engagement and closed deals.

Direct Revenue Responsibility: A core part of the job is focused on generating revenue and directly contributing to the company's bottom line.

Sales Cycle Duration: The sales activities are centred around short-term objectives, typically aligned with quarterly or annual goals.

2. Drivers / Key Performance Metrics

Next, identify the key performance metrics—or "drivers"—that reflect success for each sales role.

Key performance metrics, or "drivers," are quantifiable measures that reflect success for each sales role. Examples include **revenue, number of new customer acquisitions, customer retention rates**, or **contribution margin**. These should be carefully chosen to align with business outcomes and avoid overcomplication.

FOR A SALES COMPENSATION PLAN

$	(icon)	(icon)
Revenue / Sales Volume	New Customer Acquisation	Customer Retention
(icon)	ARR	(icon)
Gross Margin	Annual Recurring Revenue – ARR	Sales Cyc e Length
(icon)	(icon)	(icon)
Win Rate	Quota Attianment	Productivity

Don't come with a 'shopping list', come with the maximum 2 or 3 drivers, that really matter. These should be quantifiable, clearly aligned to overarching business outcomes, and carefully chosen to avoid over-complication. The goal is to focus salespeople on what truly matters. For example, revenue, number of new customer acquisitions, customer retention rates, or contribution margin might each serve as effective drivers depending on the role. Selecting two to three core metrics, rather than a broad list, helps ensure that salespeople can easily understand and act upon them. It also ensures that your salespeople can focus on what matters most for your business and not get distracted by a too long list of measures.

Revenue	Customer Acquisition	Retention
New Biz	New Biz	Account Manager

3. Payment

Pay-Mix

30%

70%

■ Base ■ Target Incentive

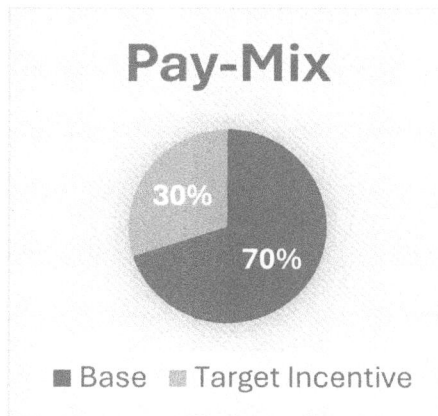

Determining the right pay-mix—how total compensation is split between base salary and variable pay—is critical. This mix should reflect both the nature of the sales role and the level of influence the individual has over outcomes. For high-impact, high-growth roles like new business development, a more aggressive mix such as 50/50 (base/variable) can be highly motivating. Conversely, roles involving long sales cycles, cross-functional collaboration, or complex solutions may require a more conservative ratio, such as 70/30, to maintain

stability. The key is to strike a balance that drives desired behaviours without undermining motivation or creating undue financial risk for the salesperson. See my earlier chapter for more details.

Pay-Mix vs. Leverage:

Pay-Mix: The mix is the relationship between the base salary and the target incentive (TI) component of target total compensation (TTC) for expected performance. The mix is expressed as a ratio of two parts of 100% (of TTC). For example, a 70/30 salary mix is a plan that has 70% of the TTC reserved in base salary while 30% of the TTC is the target incentive amount. The higher the target incentive, the higher the risk for the salesperson.

Degree of Influence

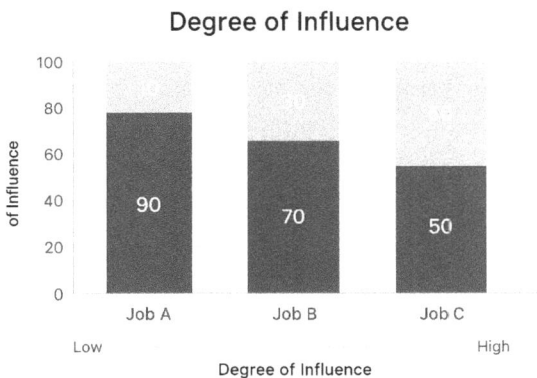

Leverage: The leverage is the total amount of incentive monies available for outstanding performance. It is expressed as a multiple of the target incentive amount. For example, a 3x leverage provides 3x the incentive amount for outstanding performance. For a 70/30 mix, the earnings potential of the best performers (90th percentile) is 3 times 30, which equals 90. For a pay plan with a TTC of $100K, the base would be $70K, the target incentive $30K and the outstanding incentive earnings would be $90K. In this scenario, poor performers would earn $70K (base pay only).

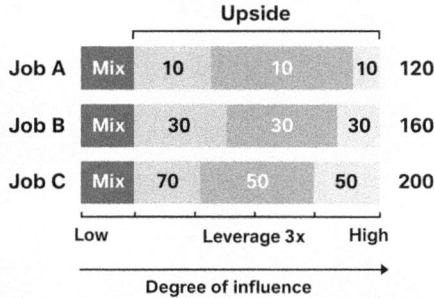

See also the Appendix for more information!

4. Trends

Modern sales environments evolve rapidly, and sales compensation plans must adapt accordingly. The rise of subscription-based business models, for instance, has introduced new metrics like Annual Recurring Revenue (ARR), customer retention rates, and Lifetime Value (LTV) into the compensation conversation. In these models, traditional commission structures based on upfront revenue may no longer be appropriate. It is important to continuously evaluate how your compensation framework aligns with current and emerging business models to remain competitive and relevant.

PAYOUT FREQUENCY ALIGNED WITH SALES CYCLES

SALES CYCLE	PAYOUT FREQUENCY
SHORT	MONTHLY
MEDIUM	QUARTERLY
LONG	BI-ANNUALLY

5. Payout Frequency

The timing of compensation payouts has a direct impact on motivation and trust. To maximize the psychological connection between effort and reward, payouts should be made as close to the sales activity as practical. Monthly payouts are ideal in fast-paced environments, while quarterly may suffice for longer sales cycles. Delays in payment can create financial stress for salespeople and dilute the incentive effect, especially in high-pressure or quota-driven roles. Try to set up your accounting that you can pay one month after the quarter ended, if quarterly payments are best for your organization. The closer the payment happens to the event of closing a deal, the more memorable it is for your salespeople. They will like the feeling that they get when seeing their payslip and will want to repeat this

6. Target Setting

Setting appropriate targets or quotas is essential to ensure that the compensation plan is both motivating and achievable. Quotas should be grounded in historical data, market potential, and capacity planning. They should also be tailored across different sales geographies, industries, or experience levels. This could mean implementing uplift factors for high-performing territories, adjusting quotas based on market maturity, or providing tiered targets for ramping sales reps. A well-thought-out target-setting process supports fairness, encourages consistent performance, and helps lead to overall business predictability.

7. Communication and Rollout

Even the best-designed compensation plan will fall short without clear and strategic communication. Salespeople must understand how it works, how they earn rewards, and how their efforts tie to business outcomes. Salespeople must understand how the plan works, how they earn their incentives, and what actions will lead to success. A strong rollout includes clear documentation, role-specific training sessions, and an open channel for questions and feedback. Transparency breeds trust, and trust is essential for adoption. If salespeople feel informed, supported, and confident in the system, they are far more likely to engage fully and perform at a high level. Add examples, ideally real-life examples. Be very transparent in your way of communicating and repeat the training throughout the year and especially for new mid-year starters. Only if you tell all involved, what the aimed outcome is, will they be able to deliver accordingly.

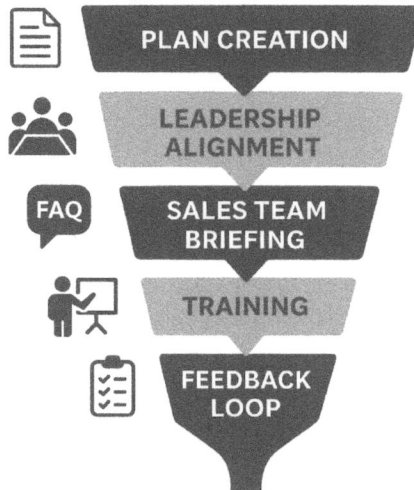

8. Governance and Compliance

A critical, often overlooked component of any sales compensation plan is the framework that ensures it operates within legal, ethical, and organizational boundaries. Governance and compliance are not just administrative concerns—they are fundamental to building trust, reducing risk, and sustaining the long-term viability of your compensation strategy. Every plan must comply with relevant labour laws, tax regulations, and—when operating across borders—varying legal standards for variable compensation in different regions or countries.

Equally important is the creation of a clear and auditable process for calculating and issuing payouts. This includes maintaining detailed documentation of how quotas are set, how performance is measured, and how earnings are calculated. There should be predefined escalation paths for addressing disputes or exceptions, so that issues are resolved fairly and consistently. Ownership of the compensation plan—whether by SalesOps, HR, or a Compensation Committee—must also be clearly defined to prevent ambiguity or inconsistency in enforcement. Establishing strong governance helps ensure your plan remains defensible under scrutiny and fosters a sense of fairness and integrity among your sales team.

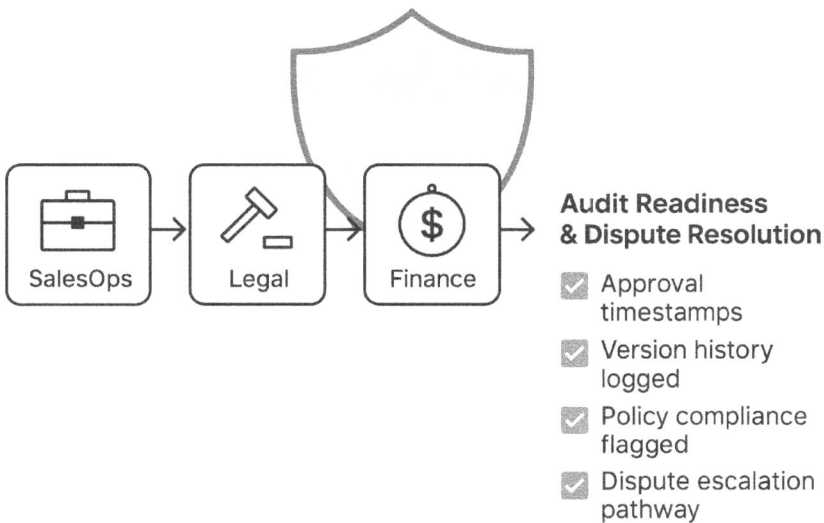

SalesOps → **Legal** → **Finance** →

Audit Readiness & Dispute Resolution

- ☑ Approval timestamps
- ☑ Version history logged
- ☑ Policy compliance flagged
- ☑ Dispute escalation pathway

9. Plan Evaluation and Iteration

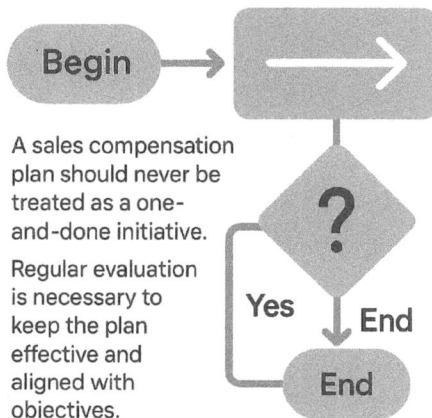

A sales compensation plan should never be treated as a one-and-done initiative. Business conditions, market dynamics, and company priorities evolve rapidly—and your compensation framework must evolve with them. Regular evaluation of the plan's performance is essential to determine whether it is driving the intended behaviours and delivering results. This means going beyond reviewing payout data and digging into how the plan influences sales strategy execution, territory coverage, team morale, and revenue mix.

A formal review cycle—conducted quarterly, semi-annually, or annually—should include input from cross-functional stakeholders such as Finance, Sales Leadership, Human Resources, and Sales Operations. It is also important to monitor for unintended consequences, such as gaming of metrics, excessive discounting, or salespeople prioritizing short-term wins over long-term growth. These behavioural distortions often surface gradually and can erode value over time. The best organizations build feedback loops into their compensation strategy, using performance data, sales rep feedback, and manager insights to refine and recalibrate the plan. Iteration ensures your plan remains effective, competitive, and aligned with both strategic objectives and frontline realities.

PLAN EVALUATION AND ITERATION

Begin →

A sales compensation plan should never be treated as a one-and-done initiative.

Regular evaluation is necessary to keep the plan effective and aligned with objectives.

?

Yes

End

End

10. Tools, Systems & Automation

The effectiveness of any sales compensation plan depends heavily on the systems and tools used to support it. As plans become more sophisticated—with multiple roles, custom quotas, and diverse performance metrics—manual processes are no longer sufficient. Investing in the right technology is essential for ensuring accuracy, transparency, and scalability.

Sales Performance Management (SPM) platforms and CRM-integrated tools allow for real-time tracking of sales progress, automated calculation of incentives, and consistent application of plan rules. These systems reduce administrative burden and eliminate errors that can undermine salespeople trust in the plan. They also provide visibility to salespeople, who can monitor their own progress against targets and estimate upcoming payouts. This immediacy reinforces the motivational power of the incentive structure. Additionally, automated systems make it easier to adapt the plan mid-year, run scenario analyses, and align compensation mechanics with dynamic changes in the sales environment. Without the right infrastructure in place, even the most well-designed plans can falter in execution.

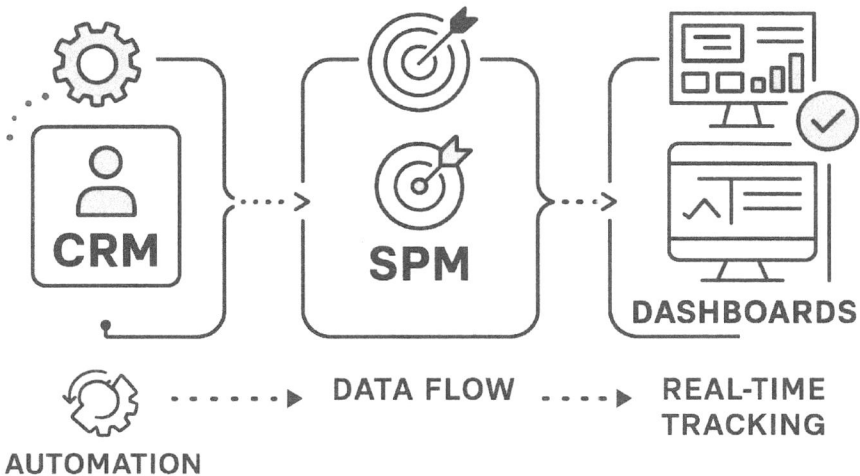

CRM · · · · > SPM · · · > DASHBOARDS

AUTOMATION · · · · · · > DATA FLOW · · · · > REAL-TIME TRACKING

11. Behavioural Economics & Motivation Psychology

While numbers, metrics, and financial models form the foundation of a compensation plan, the real motivator of success lies in human behaviour. Understanding what truly motivates people—and designing compensation accordingly—is essential to unlocking discretionary effort and sustained performance. Incorporating insights from behavioural economics and psychology transforms a compensation plan from a financial model into a motivational engine. Effective sales compensation plans speak not only to logic, but to emotion—creating momentum, ownership, and a deeper sense of purpose.

For example, structuring rewards around frequent, tangible wins can be more motivating than a single large payout at year's end. Leveraging concepts like loss aversion—where people work harder to avoid losing a reward than to gain one—can be a powerful psychological tool. Recognizing milestones, celebrating top performers, and introducing gamified elements like leaderboards or SPIFs (Sales Performance Incentive Funds) can also amplify engagement. Beyond cash, non-monetary incentives such as recognition, career advancement, or unique experiences often hold disproportionate motivational value.

Ultimately, a great sales compensation plan is as much about how it makes people *feel* as it is about what it pays. When salespeople feel ownership, clarity, and a sense of momentum, they are far more likely to exceed expectations. Embedding behavioural design principles into your plan ensures that it not only aligns with your strategy but also resonates with the people who bring it to life.

RATIONAL DRIVERS   MOTIVATIONAL
TRIGGERS

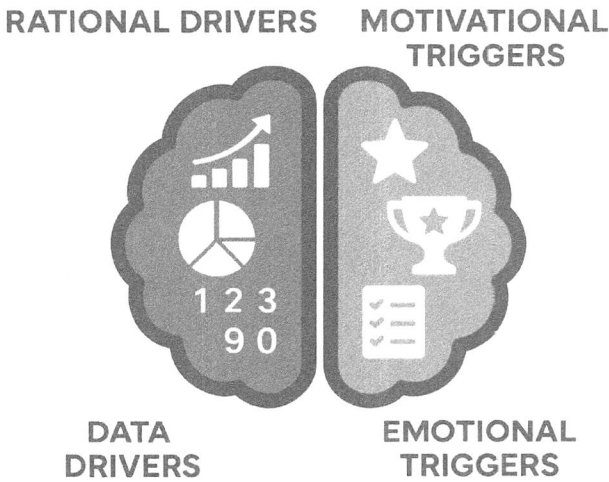

DATA   EMOTIONAL
DRIVERS   TRIGGERS

Case Study: A Successful Compensation Rollout

A mid-sized technology company was grappling with stalled growth and declining morale among its sales team. Quota attainment was inconsistent, turnover was rising, and salespeople expressed frustration with a sales compensation structure that felt misaligned with their efforts and unclear in its expectations.

To address the issue, company leadership undertook a comprehensive seven-step compensation redesign. This process began with a deep dive into sales roles and responsibilities, leading to the implementation of differentiated, role-based compensation plans. These plans acknowledged the unique contributions of each sales function—whether hunting, farming, or account management—and tailored incentives accordingly.

The company then streamlined performance metrics, reducing clutter and focusing on KPIs that truly drove business outcomes. This not only simplified plan communication but also made it easier for sales reps to understand how their actions translated to earnings. Greater transparency was introduced through regular plan reviews and open Q&A sessions, helping to build trust and buy-in across the team.

Another key move was adjusting the pay-mix to better reflect the company's sales cycle. For example, those in longer, consultative sales roles received a higher base-to-variable ratio, while inside sales reps working on shorter cycles had more aggressive variable incentives to result in speed and volume. These adjustments ensured that compensation was both motivating and realistic based on the nature of the sale.

The results were clear and compelling. Within six months of rollout, the company experienced a 25% increase in overall quota attainment, a 15% lift in net-new revenue, and a notable uptick in sales rep satisfaction, as measured by internal engagement surveys. Sales leaders reported more productive pipeline conversations, and sales teams demonstrated higher focus and confidence in hitting their targets.

Ultimately, the success of this initiative came down to three things: clarity in plan design, consistency in execution, and strategic alignment between compensation and business goals. By treating compensation as a lever for performance—not just a payout mechanism—the company reinvigorated its sales force and set a stronger foundation for scalable growth.

——— CONCLUSION ———

A well-designed sales compensation plan is not a static document—it is a dynamic, evolving strategy that must grow alongside your business. When built thoughtfully, it becomes a powerful connector between high-level business objectives and day-to-day sales execution. By taking a structured, intentional approach to plan design, you ensure that incentives align with priorities, encourage the right behaviours, and ultimately drive sustainable performance and long-term impact.

THE 3-WIN STRATEGY
Sales Compensation in Harmony

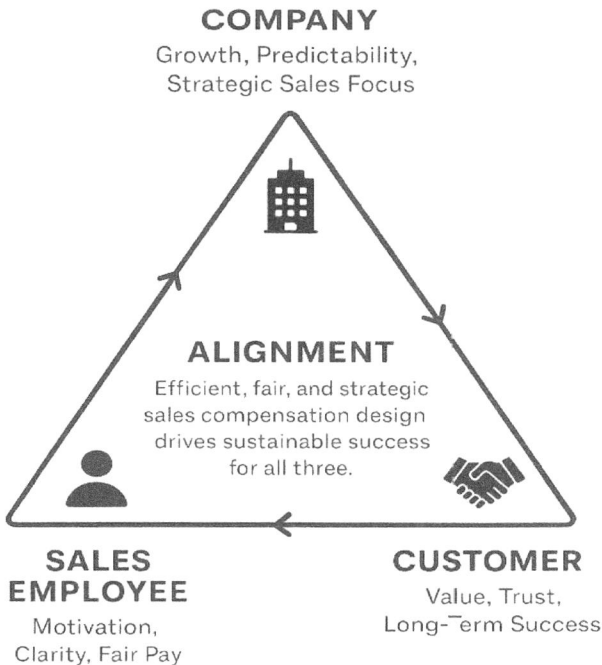

COMPANY
Growth, Predictability,
Strategic Sales Focus

ALIGNMENT
Efficient, fair, and strategic
sales compensation design
drives sustainable success
for all three.

SALES EMPLOYEE
Motivation,
Clarity, Fair Pay

CUSTOMER
Value, Trust,
Long-Term Success

A truly effective sales compensation plan creates a **3-Win outcome**—a strategic alignment where the **company**, the **salesperson**, and the **customer** all benefit simultaneously.

When plans are **clear, fair, and strategically aligned**, this alignment becomes self-reinforcing:

- ▶ The **company** wins by driving the right sales behaviours, achieving revenue goals, and supporting long-term growth.
- ▶ The **sales employee** wins by being fairly compensated, motivated, and empowered to perform at their best.
- ▶ The **customer** wins by experiencing a consultative, needs-based sales process—delivered by motivated sales representatives who are focused on solving real problems, not just closing deals.

This harmony ensures that incentives are not at odds, but rather mutually reinforcing—leading to sustained performance, stronger relationships, and lasting business value.

CHAPTER 5

Compensation Models

Understanding Different Compensation Models

Different sales compensation models shape different sales behaviours - choose wisely.

> **What design elements are essential to create a sales compensation plan that motivates the right behaviours?**

Problem: Companies frequently select a compensation model without evaluating its influence on sales behaviour or overall strategy, resulting in an ineffective and unmotivating sales plan.

Result: The right model fosters motivation, efficiency, and alignment with company goals.

- Commission Rate vs. Pay-Mix Base Salary & Commission vs. KPI Plan vs. Hybrid Model
- Selecting the right measures to link to your company strategy that drives the right behaviour. Keep it simple!
- Linking measures to strategy
- Tiered and Accelerated Commissions – When and how to use them.
- The role of AI and automation in sales compensation.

Real-World Example: How companies tailor sales compensation models to business needs

Learnings: After reading this chapter, you will understand how to identify what compensation model best works for you and why it is important to select wisely. You will understand, which compensation models are driving the right behaviours.

First of all: What do we mean when we talk about a compensation model? A compensation model is the structured framework a company uses to determine how employees—especially salespeople—are paid. It defines the mix of base salary, incentives (like commissions or bonuses), and other financial rewards based on performance. In sales, the compensation model directly influences how sales representatives behave, what they prioritize, and how they align with business goals.

In simple terms: It is the blueprint for how pay is earned—whether someone gets paid more for closing new deals, retaining customers, selling certain products, hitting revenue targets, or all of the above.

Why It matters: The compensation model isn't just about paying people—it guides behaviour. A well-designed model motivates the right actions (e.g. quality sales, customer retention), while a poor model can lead to short-term wins, misaligned priorities, or even burnout.

Sales compensation is not a one-size-fits-all discipline. The model you choose has a direct impact on how your sales team behaves, what they prioritize, and how well they align with company objectives. Each structure sends a signal to your salesforce about what matters most. That is why selecting the right compensation model is more than a financial decision—it is a strategic one that shapes your entire go-to-market execution.

This chapter explores the different compensation models available, the psychological and strategic signals they send, and how they can either reinforce or derail a company's growth objectives. Selecting the right model is not a matter of preference or tradition; it is a deliberate decision that reflects what your company values are, how your sales motion works, and what kind of outcomes you are trying to drive.

Many companies choose a compensation model based on familiarity, competitor actions, or ease of implementation, without evaluating the impact on behaviour or strategic outcomes. The result is often a misaligned, de-motivating plan that rewards the wrong actions and fails to generate consistent performance. For example, an overemphasis on commission without consideration for role complexity or customer lifecycle may result in a team that chases quick wins while ignoring customer retention, profitability, or long-term value creation. The outcome? Misalignment, lack of focus, and a sales culture that rewards the wrong actions.

When thoughtfully chosen and clearly communicated, the right compensation model boosts motivation, sharpens focus, and ensures alignment with both sales roles and company goals. It drives the behaviours that matter most—whether that is landing new deals, expanding existing accounts, improving customer retention or all of it—while giving salespeople a clear and fair path to success. They energize the sales team, clarify goals, and provide a roadmap for success. Salespeople understand what is expected of them and how their performance contributes to the bigger picture—whether that is acquiring new customers, growing existing accounts, or improving customer satisfaction. This level of alignment creates purpose, enhances motivation, and leads to more predictable, consistent performance across the organization.

Commission Rate vs. Pay-Mix Models

There are several common compensation structures, each with different strengths:

Comparative Table of Compensation Models

Model	Ideal For	Pros	Cons	Sales Cycle
Straight Commission	High-volume transactional sales	High motivation, low fixed cost	Risk of short-term focus	Short
Base + Commission	Mid-complexity, longer cycle sales	Balanced, motivational	Requires good quota setting	Medium

Model	Ideal For	Pros	Cons	Sales Cycle
KPI-Based	Multi-role outcomes, CS roles	Aligns with strategy, holistic	Harder to measure accurately	Varies
Hybrid	Enterprise, consultative sales	Flexibility, role-tailored	Complex to manage	Long

Choosing the right model depends on your industry, sales motion, sales cycle length, and company maturity.

At the heart of any compensation system is its structural foundation—how pay is divided between fixed and variable components, and how success is measured. Different models shape different behaviours. A straight commission model, for instance, is high-risk and high-reward, and tends to push for aggressive pursuit of new business, often suited for transactional sales with short cycles. A base salary plus sales commission (pay-mix) model offers more balance, appealing to roles where a level of stability is required but performance incentives are still critical. KPI-based plans, meanwhile, broaden the scope of measurement by tying rewards to a set of strategic performance indicators—ideal for roles that impact customer experience, retention, or upselling.

Hybrid models combine these elements and are increasingly common in organizations with complex or multi-faceted sales roles. For example, a hybrid plan might offer base salary, commission on revenue, and bonuses tied to account health or renewal rates. The key is selecting a structure that fits the nature of your sales cycle, the behaviours you want to encourage, and the maturity of your business model. No model is universally best—only the one that best supports your specific goals.

To summarize: Selecting the right compensation structure is foundational to influencing how your sales team operates and what they focus on. A commission-only model typically works best in environments where the sales cycle is short, the product is transactional, and the salesperson has full control over the buying decision. It encourages hustle, self-direction, and a sharp focus on closing deals—but it can also lead to short-term thinking and neglect of relationship-building. A pay-mix model, where compensation is split between a base salary and commission, offers greater stability and appeals to roles that require nurturing longer-term relationships or complex deal navigation. KPI-based plans go a step further by tying compensation to specific, non-revenue performance metrics such as customer satisfaction, deal quality, or compliance with sales processes. Hybrid models combine elements of all three approaches and are particularly useful in businesses with varying sales motions or product lines, offering flexibility to adapt compensation to different go-to-market strategies.

Category	Straight Commission	Base + Commission	KPI-Based	Hybrid Model
Works well for	Fast, transactional sales; short cycles	Longer or relationship-driven deals	Roles tied to quality, process, or satisfaction metrics	Teams with mixed roles or varied sales motions
Pros	High drive; low fixed cost	Stability; supports long-term focus	Aligns behaviour to broader goals	Flexible; adaptable to multiple strategies
Cons	Short-term focus; income swings	Lower urgency; higher fixed cost	Hard to track; may confuse priorities	Complex to manage; risk of overlap

Behavioural Economics Insight:

Behavioural psychology explains why certain structures motivate more than others:

- **Goal Gradient Effect**: Accelerators work because people are more motivated as they approach a visible target.
- **Loss Aversion**: Sales representatives fear losing bonus potential more than they're excited by gains.
- **Variable Reward**: Changing commission tiers can stimulate dopamine-based motivation, like a slot machine.

71

Pitfalls to Avoid

- Overcomplicating KPI models with more than 3 metrics
- Using identical plans for different roles
- Misaligning payout with long-term value creation
- Ignoring plan effectiveness post-implementation

Global Considerations Compensation models must often adapt to:

- Local labour laws (e.g., commission caps)
- Norms around bonuses vs. fixed pay
- Currency volatility and inflation effects

Evolving Compensation as You Scale Your plan must grow with you:

- **Startup phase**: Lean toward commission-heavy to drive early growth.
- **Growth phase**: Hybrid models that stabilize and align efforts.
- **Enterprise phase**: KPI-based, highly tailored, and role-specific plans.

KPI-Based Model — Do's and Don'ts

Do:

- Use a few meaningful, easy-to-track KPIs
- Match KPIs to role objectives (e.g., CS = retention)

Don't:

- Include vanity metrics (e.g., call volume for senior reps)
- Frequently change KPIs unless justified by strategy

Real-Life Example: For example, a CRM company —a leader in inbound marketing and CRM software—adopted a hybrid compensation approach. Their sales roles span transactional inside sales, mid-market growth, and enterprise consultative selling. They found that a one-size-fits-all model didn't work. By creating role-specific plans with a mix of commission, base salary, and KPIs, they incentivized sales reps to focus on what mattered for their segment, from closing new logos to reducing churn and driving cross-sell success.

Linking Measures to Strategy

One of the most important principles in compensation design is strategic alignment. Your sales compensation plan should reflect what your company is trying to achieve—whether that is rapid growth, entering new markets, driving profitability, or increasing customer lifetime value. The chosen performance measures should reinforce those objectives directly.

That said, simplicity is critical. Overloading plans with too many metrics can dilute focus, confuse sales teams, and lead to scattered performance. The most effective compensation plans identify the one to three core metrics that matter most for each role. For a new business sales representative, that might be annual contract value (ACV) or net-new logos. For a customer success manager, it might be renewal rates or upsell revenue. Each metric should be a clear expression of the role's strategic purpose.

Effective compensation models are linked clearly to strategic business priorities. Whether your company is focused on revenue growth, market expansion, customer retention, or profitability, your measures must support that goal. Focused plans are key—avoid overcomplicating plans with too many metrics. Instead, focus on the 1–3 most important drivers of success for each role.

A sales compensation plan is only as effective as the performance metrics it reinforces. The most successful companies start by asking what strategic behaviours they need to drive—and then work backwards to select a few, meaningful metrics that reflect those behaviours. Clarity is vital; overcomplicating the plan with too many targets can confuse the sales team, dilute focus, and create misaligned execution. Instead, well-designed plans isolate the top one to three outcomes that truly define success for each role. These could include revenue, margin, customer retention, net new acquisition, or specific product mix—whatever best reflects the company's growth strategy and market position.

Real-Life Example: A strong example of this comes from Zendesk, a customer service platform. As the company moved from a single product offering to a broader suite, it had to shift its compensation structure to promote multi-product adoption. Rather than adding dozens of KPIs, Zendesk focused its sales compensation plans on just two key metrics: upsell revenue from existing clients and product mix diversification. This focus helped streamline sales conversations and ensured sales representatives were aligned with the company's broader goal of platform adoption.

Tiered and Accelerated Commissions

Tiered and accelerated commission structures are powerful tools when used strategically:

- ▶ **Tiered Commissions** reward progressively higher performance with increased rates as sales reps hit new thresholds.
- ▶ **Accelerators** add momentum by significantly boosting payout once targets are surpassed, keeping top performers engaged and driving overperformance.

Both mechanisms can push sales reps to stretch beyond quota, but they must be calibrated carefully to avoid overpayment or misaligned incentives.

Tiered and accelerated commission structures add another layer of motivation, especially for experienced and high-performing sales representatives. These tools reward salespeople progressively as they surpass performance thresholds, creating a sense of momentum and urgency. For example, a salesperson may earn a base commission rate up to 100% of quota and then receive a higher rate for any revenue beyond that. Accelerators go even further boosting the payout significantly once certain targets are exceeded.

Used wisely, these mechanisms can transform average performance into overperformance by incentivizing salespeople to stretch their efforts. But they must be calibrated carefully to avoid unintended consequences, such as gaming the system, sandbagging, or overpaying for deals that don't contribute to long-term value.

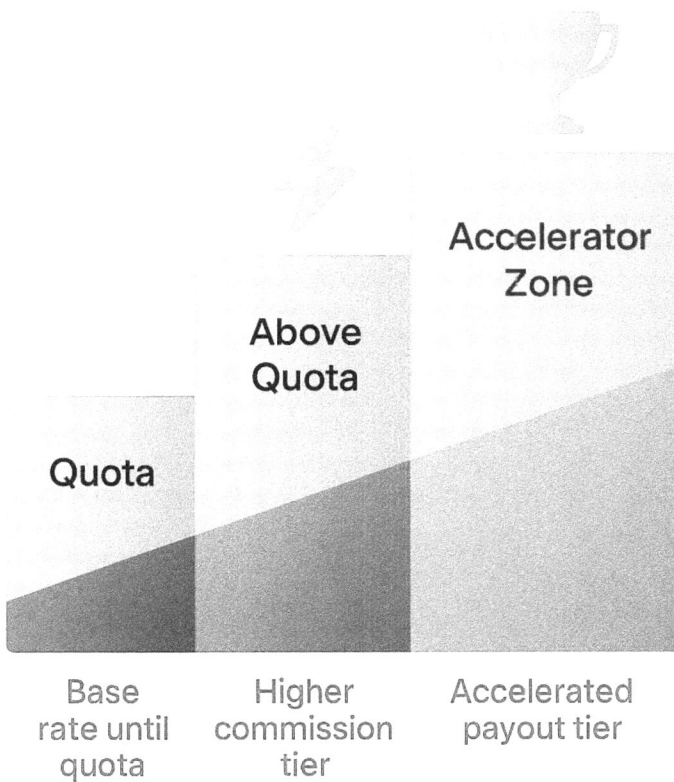

Real-Life Example: A compelling real-life case is Cisco Systems. To drive sales during a major product launch, Cisco implemented a tiered and accelerated structure that offered increasing commission rates as sales reps sold more units of the new product. The plan was temporary, aligned with the product's launch phase, and highly targeted. The result was a massive uptake in early adoption, hitting both revenue and market share goals. Importantly, once the momentum was established, Cisco scaled the plan back to a more standard structure, avoiding long-term cost inflation.

AI and Automation in Compensation Planning

With modern tools, sales compensation planning is becoming smarter and more responsive:

▶ **AI and automation** can analyse performance trends, recommend adjustments to pay structures, and even detect early signs of plan ineffectiveness.

▶ These technologies allow for faster iteration, personalised goal setting, and more transparent compensation processes—freeing up time and reducing disputes.

The result is a more agile, data-driven approach that keeps compensation plans aligned with real-time business needs.

Modern compensation planning is no longer just a finance or HR function—it is increasingly powered by data and technology. Artificial intelligence and automation are now being used to enhance fairness, agility, and effectiveness in sales compensation. These tools can identify trends, simulate plan outcomes, and provide early warnings when incentive structures aren't producing the intended results.

AI-driven tools can also personalize compensation targets, recommend quota adjustments, or optimize pay-mix models based on real-time business conditions. This makes the planning process more responsive and more transparent, reducing disputes and freeing leadership to focus on strategy rather than administration. For organizations with large or global salesforces, the value of automation cannot be overstated—it improves governance, accuracy, and the ability to adapt plans in a fast-changing market.

AI and Automation in Compensation Planning

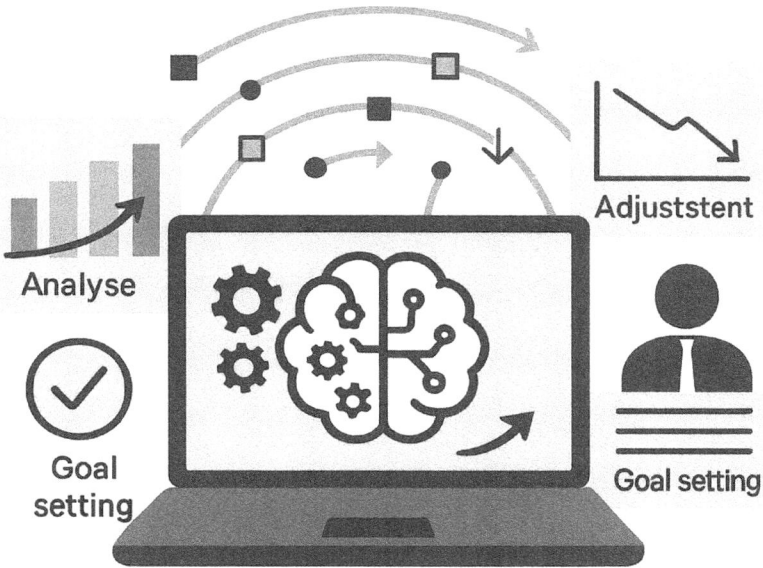

Analyse

Adjuststent

Goal setting

Goal setting

With modern tools, sales compensation planning is becoming smarter and more responsive.

- AI and automation can analyse performance trends, recommend adjustrrients, and detect sarly signs of plan ineffectiveness
- Transparent goal setting approach

Real-Life Example: Take IBM, for instance. The tech giant has incorporated AI into its compensation planning through its internal Watson AI platform. IBM uses data from sales CRM, HR systems, and market analytics to continuously refine compensation models, identify underperforming plans, and suggest tailored incentives. This approach not only improved plan efficiency and reduced administrative overhead but also increased sales productivity by ensuring sales representatives had personalized, data-informed goals and incentives that matched real-time market dynamics.

Real-Life Example: Tailoring Models to Business Needs

A global software company with multiple product lines needed different compensation approaches for each. For fast-moving, transactional products, they used a commission-heavy model with weekly payouts and accelerators. For complex enterprise solutions, they shifted to a hybrid model—blending base salary, deal-based bonuses, and KPIs like implementation quality and customer satisfaction. This tailored approach improved both sales results and internal collaboration, aligning performance with each product's unique value cycle.

What they did is: Firstly, recognizing that one compensation model couldn't effectively serve all sales motions, the company implemented different models for different teams. For their transactional products, salespeople were given aggressive commission plans with weekly payouts and accelerators to support rapid sales and frequent deal flow. In contrast, for strategic enterprise solutions requiring longer sales cycles and deeper customer engagement, the company adopted a hybrid model. These sales reps received a base salary, plus deal-based bonuses tied to implementation success and customer satisfaction scores.

The result was improved performance across the board—faster deal velocity for transactional products and deeper customer relationships in complex solution sales. More importantly, each team had a compensation plan that reflected the nature of their role and aligned with the company's broader strategic goals.

Case Study Walkthrough Scenario: A SaaS startup shifting to scale-up. Old Plan: 100% commission-only, flat rate. Challenges: Short-term deals, high churn, low collaboration. New Plan: Role-based hybrid model with:

- AE: Base + revenue commission + cross-sell bonus
- CS: Base + renewal KPI + churn reduction metric

Outcome: Revenue retention rose 22%, sales team engagement improved, and fewer customer escalations.

CONCLUSION

The structure of your sales compensation model is one of the most influential levers you have to drive performance, focus behaviour, and achieve strategic outcomes. When compensation aligns with your sales process, company goals, and role expectations, it becomes a source of clarity, purpose, and motivation. But when it is misaligned, it can quickly become a source of frustration and inefficiency.

The key to success is thoughtful design: selecting the right model, linking it to your strategy, adapting it as the company evolves, and ensuring it speaks clearly to the sales behaviours you want to promote. Compensation doesn't just pay your salespeople—it shapes how they think, act, and succeed.

CHAPTER 6

Pitfalls & Mistakes

Common Pitfalls & How to Avoid Them (incl. Mid-Year Changes & Conflict of Purpose, 10% Measures / Pay-mix)

Avoiding common sales compensation mistakes helps save money, retains top talent, boosts morale and maintains strategic alignment.

> **What are the biggest mistakes in sales compensation plans, and how can you prevent them?**

Problem: Poorly designed sales compensation plans can demotivate high performers, cause conflicts, and result in overpayment or underpayment.

Result: Avoiding these pitfalls ensures a fair, competitive, and scalable compensation structure that attracts, retains, and motivates top sales talent.

- ▶ Overpaying or underpaying sales reps.
- ▶ Mid-Year plan changes & conflicts of purpose.
- ▶ Demotivating high performers,
- ▶ Misalignment between sales and company objectives.

Case Study: How a company lost top talent due to a poorly designed sales compensation plan.

Learnings: After reading this chapter, you will be equipped to identify potential challenges at an early stage, enabling you to proactively avoid common pitfalls that can hinder sales performance. You will also develop a structured approach for implementing corrective actions when deviations occur and gain a comprehensive understanding of the essential role that testing and modelling play in refining and validating your sales strategy.

Avoiding common sales compensation mistakes helps save money, retain top talent, boosts morale, and maintains strategic alignment. Getting sales compensation right is not just about motivating performance—it is about building a system that safeguards long-term business health.

Common Sales Compensation Pitfalls

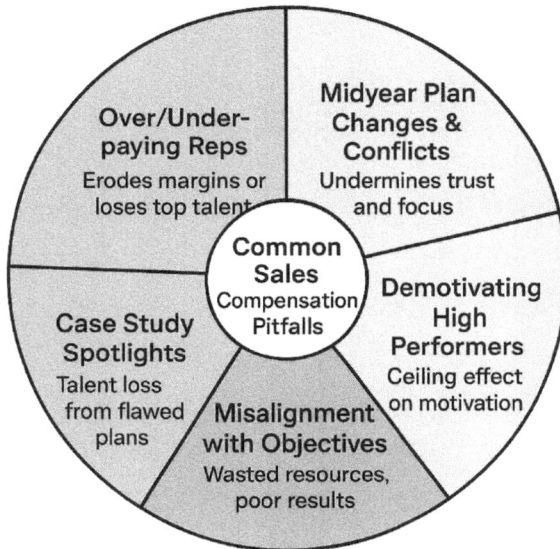

Poorly designed compensation plans introduce friction, erode trust, and often produce inconsistent or unintended behaviours. Worse still, these issues usually surface only after damage has been done—whether through lost talent, financial inefficiencies, or misaligned execution.

Compensation that seems effective on the surface can quietly damage your culture, drain your budget, and push your top performers out the door. A poorly designed plan introduces unnecessary friction, creates ambiguity, and often leads to inconsistent or unintended behaviours. What makes it worse is that these issues are often discovered only after results suffer or key talent leaves. This chapter explores the most damaging pitfalls and, more importantly, how to avoid them with foresight and data-driven decision-making.

One of the most common, yet costly, mistakes in sales compensation is either overpaying or underpaying sales reps. Overpayment often happens when commission structures are too generous for deals that contribute little to long-term profitability, such as one-time hardware sales or unsustainable discounts. This erodes margin without delivering sustained value.

Conversely, underpayment—especially of top-performing salespeople— sends a signal that excellence isn't recognized or fairly rewarded. This creates disillusionment and opens the door for competitors to poach your best people. Getting the balance right requires rigorous testing and calibration of your pay-mix, performance thresholds, and commission curves. Data should be your guide—not gut feel or legacy structures.

This chapter explores the most damaging compensation pitfalls and how to avoid them through thoughtful design, foresight, and data-driven decision-making.

Quantifying the exact costs associated with rectifying errors in sales compensation plan design can be challenging, as these expenses vary significantly based on factors such as company size, industry, and geographic region and are not always public. However, available data and industry insights provide a general understanding of the potential financial impact:

Administrative and Operational Costs

Companies that rely on manual processes for managing sales compensation plans often face increased administrative burdens. For instance, organizations using spreadsheets may spend up to six weeks processing compensation payouts. Errors in these processes can further extend this timeframe, leading to decreased productivity as sales representatives engage in "shadow accounting" to verify their commissions.

Impact on Sales Performance

Ineffective compensation plans can demotivate sales teams. A survey of over 450 professionals in the technology sector revealed that 91% of organizations had less than 80% of their sales representatives meeting quotas, with compensation plan issues cited as a significant factor.

Turnover and Recruitment Expenses

Poorly designed compensation structures can lead to higher turnover rates among top-performing sales personnel. Replacing these individuals incurs costs related to recruitment, training, and lost sales opportunities during the transition period.

Regional and Company Size Considerations

While specific cost breakdowns by region and company size are not readily available, it is generally observed that larger enterprises may face higher absolute costs due to the scale of their sales operations. Conversely, smaller companies might experience a more significant relative impact, as they often have limited resources to address and rectify compensation plan issues.

Legal Risks

Oracle – $150 Million Class Action Over Retroactive Commission Cuts: In 2017, Oracle faced a class action lawsuit filed by former sales representative Marcella Johnson. The suit alleged that Oracle retroactively altered commission agreements—referred to as "re-planning"—to reduce commissions on past sales, sometimes even reclaiming payments already made. This practice affected an estimated 1,000 to 2,000 salespeople and was claimed to violate California labour laws.

Wells Fargo – Class Action Over Sales Quotas and Compensation: In 2016, two former Wells Fargo employees filed a class action lawsuit alleging that they were penalized for not meeting unrealistic sales quotas. The suit claimed that employees who refused to engage in fraudulent activities to meet these quotas were demoted, fired, or forced to resign, and sought $2.6 billion in compensation for affected employees.

Westgate Resorts – Unpaid Sales Commissions: In 2010, 300 former sales employees sued Westgate Resorts for unpaid sales commissions. The lawsuit resulted in a judgment ordering Westgate to pay $600,000. However, after initial payments, Westgate ceased further payments, leading to additional legal proceedings. The matter was eventually settled, with Westgate agreeing to pay $500,000. BTW...they counter-sued!

Australia: Appco Group Class Action: Appco Group, a subsidiary of The Cobra Group, faced an $85 million class action lawsuit in Australia over alleged underpayment and exploitation of sales workers. The plaintiffs accused the company of misleading compensation promises and subjecting workers to humiliating practices. This case has been described as one of the most significant underpayment disputes in Australian history.

Germany: Equal Pay for Sales Representatives: The German Federal Labour Court addressed a case where a female sales representative received a lower salary than her male counterparts for the same role. The employer contended that the male employee had negotiated better terms. The court dismissed this argument, stating that negotiation skills do not justify pay disparities for identical work, and awarded the plaintiff €14,000 in back pay and €2,000 in compensation.

It can also go the other way:

Wells Fargo Cross-Selling Scandal: Between 2011 and 2016, Wells Fargo terminated approximately 5,300 employees for creating millions of unauthorized accounts to meet aggressive sales targets. While the company initially blamed lower-level employees, investigations revealed that the fraudulent activities were driven by top-down pressure to meet unrealistic sales quotas. Although specific lawsuits against individual employees for overpaid commissions were not widely publicized, the bank's actions included terminations and internal disciplinary measures.

Koehl v. Verio, Inc. (California, 2006): In this case, Verio, Inc. sought to recover advance commission payments from sales associates when sales did not materialize as expected. The court upheld the company's right to reclaim unearned commissions, emphasizing that the employees had agreed to the terms outlined in the compensation plan, which included provisions for chargebacks if certain conditions were not met.

Recommendations

To mitigate these costs:

- ▶ **Automate Compensation Processes**: Implementing sales performance management software can reduce errors and administrative time.
- ▶ **Regularly Review Compensation Plans**: Periodic assessments ensure that plans remain aligned with company goals and market conditions.
- ▶ **Engage Stakeholders in Plan Design**: Involving sales representatives and managers can lead to more effective and motivating compensation structures. Cross-functional collaboration: Engaging finance, HR, and sales departments in the design and review of compensation plans can enhance accuracy and effectiveness.

Overpaying or Underpaying Sales Reps

One of the most fundamental mistakes is an imbalanced payout structure—either overpaying for low-value deals or underpaying top performers. Overpayment often results from plans that reward total revenue volume without considering deal profitability or customer lifetime value. Salespeople may be incentivized to pursue high-volume but low-margin sales that do little to support sustainable growth.

On the other end of the spectrum, underpayment is equally damaging, especially when high performers realize that their effort does not translate into fair financial recognition. Top sales reps thrive in environments where their contributions are rewarded proportionally, but if compensation structures fail to support them, they quickly disengage, leading to decreased productivity and eventual attrition.

Conversely, underpayment—especially of top performers—leads to demotivation and opens the door for competitors to poach your best people. Salespeople who feel their effort isn't being recognized disengage or leave.

Striking the right balance requires detailed modelling, frequent reviews, and the willingness to adapt the plan based on both financial data and frontline feedback.

Addressing these challenges requires careful compensation modelling and continuous testing. Sales leaders must conduct periodic pay-mix assessments to ensure the plan does not incentivize behaviours that drain company resources or discourage high-value work. By establishing clear commission tiers based on deal quality, companies can create a balanced structure that neither overpays nor underpays. Further, implementing incentives for high margin deals and penalizing excessive discounting ensures that commission payouts align with company growth objectives. Without proper financial guardrails, sales compensation plans can unintentionally encourage behaviours that conflict with long-term profitability, creating an unsustainable cycle of revenue fluctuations and talent loss.

Achieving balance requires:

- ▶ Rigorous modelling of deal economics.
- ▶ Regular reviews of commission curves.
- ▶ Tiered incentives that favour high-margin deals.
- ▶ Guardrails against excessive discounting.

Real-Life Example: A fast-growing IT services firm implemented a commission structure that heavily rewarded volume but ignored deal profitability. One sales rep closed several large contracts with low-margin pricing just to hit targets. He earned more than double the commission of peers who brought in fewer but more profitable deals. By the end of the fiscal year, finance flagged the imbalance, and two senior account managers—who had driven high-quality revenue—left the company, feeling undervalued. The company later overhauled the compensation plan to include margin thresholds, but the talent loss was already done.

Mid-Year Plan Changes & Conflicts of Purpose

Mid-year compensation changes can backfire when rolled out abruptly. While adapting to market shifts is necessary, frequent or poorly communicated changes undermine trust and destabilize motivation.

Sales representatives rely on clear and predictable compensation frameworks to plan their efforts strategically, but when mid-year revisions unexpectedly alter quotas, commission structures, or acceleration rules, frustration follows. A particular issue arises when leadership adjusts compensation metrics without properly aligning them with new business priorities. For example, if leadership shifts focus from new customer acquisition to account expansion mid-year, but the compensation plan still rewards new deals, sales teams continue prioritizing initial transactions rather than long-term customer growth. This creates internal misalignment, leading to inconsistent execution of strategic objectives.

How to mitigate:

- ▸ Model changes thoroughly before rollout.
- ▸ Communicate early and clearly.
- ▸ Use transition bonuses to cushion impact.
- ▸ Align all stakeholders—sales, finance, and leadership.

Real-Life Example: One company that fell into this trap was a SaaS provider that modified its compensation plan mid-year to emphasize gross margins over total contract value. In theory, this seemed like a sound financial strategy, but in execution, it had disastrous consequences. The company removed accelerators that had previously rewarded high-value deals, introducing stricter quota requirements while failing to account for a downturn in inbound leads. Sales reps struggled to meet their targets under the new plan, seeing their earnings drop significantly despite maintaining the same level of effort. The sudden financial instability caused widespread dissatisfaction among top performers, leading to several high-profile departures. Many reps took their customer relationships elsewhere, directly benefiting competitors. The company attempted to revert back to its old plan after realizing the negative impact, but the damage had already weakened its talent pool and reputation.

Demotivating High Performers

High performers are the backbone of any successful sales team, and their motivation is directly linked to how well compensation structures reward excellence. However, many sales organizations inadvertently demotivate their best sellers by introducing artificial earning caps, overly complex quota systems, or unclear commission structures. Without proper incentives, high achievers lose the motivation to go above and beyond, shifting their focus toward minimum targets rather than stretching for ambitious wins. The absence of proper acceleration mechanisms further exacerbates this issue. Accelerators allow top performers to earn higher commissions for exceeding quota, but when removed or poorly structured, they create a ceiling effect that discourages extra effort.

The solution lies in maintaining scalable rewards and clear performance-based acceleration systems. Compensation plans should not just reward base-level quota attainment; they should encourage continuous success by offering increased commissions for exceeding targets.

Earnings Trajectory: Cap vs. Accelerators

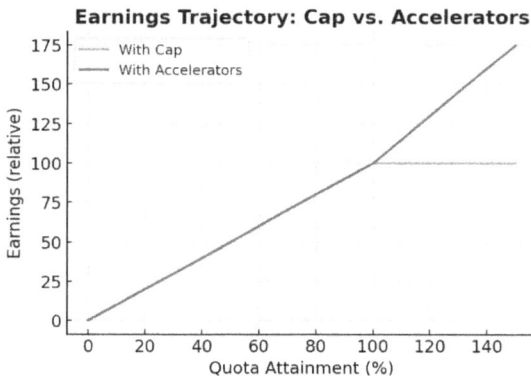

Companies should also be mindful of territory distribution and fair quota assignments, ensuring that top performers have opportunities to stretch their abilities without unnecessary structural barriers. A well-designed plan, that is professionally financially modelled, fosters a high-performance culture where effort correlates directly with reward, preventing disengagement and talent loss.

Talent Loss Timeline

Plan Change — Earnings Drop — Frustration — Resignation — Accounts Lost — Competitor Gain

Designing for motivation means:

▸ Keeping accelerators intact.
▸ Avoiding arbitrary caps.
▸ Ensuring quotas are fair and stretchable.
▸ Rewarding consistent overperformance.

Real-Life Example: A global SaaS company made a strategic decision to remove accelerators from its sales plan to control expenses. They assumed top reps would still perform out of habit. Within one quarter, three of the top five reps stopped prospecting new accounts once they hit quota, as there was no financial benefit in doing so. One high performer, responsible for landing a major enterprise client the previous year, left for a start-up offering a highly leveraged, uncapped plan. The cost of replacing that talent—and the lost pipeline—far outweighed the initial savings.

Misalignment Between Sales and Company Objectives

A misaligned compensation structure creates tension between sales teams and leadership, ultimately resulting in wasted resources, inconsistent revenue growth, and strategic inefficiencies. Companies must ensure that their sales goals align with broader business priorities, especially when scaling into new markets, launching new products, or shifting toward retention-based models. A common mistake is rewarding short-term wins without considering long-term business health. If sales reps are only incentivized for new logo acquisition but leadership is focused on increasing customer retention and product expansion, execution efforts will diverge, leading to poor results.

Best practices:

- ▶ Align KPIs with strategic goals (e.g., renewals, usage, profitability).
- ▶ Evolve compensation plans as priorities shift.
- ▶ Validate alignment through stakeholder feedback.

Sales Goals

Company
Strategy

Aligned
Execution

Real-Life Example: A cloud provider aimed to drive renewals and upsells but only paid reps for net-new sales. Account managers deprioritized expansion, and large accounts churned. Retention incentives were eventually added—renewal rates jumped 20%.

The key takeaway here is that compensation must reinforce business strategy rather than contradict it. By integrating retention incentives alongside new deal commissions, companies ensure balanced execution that supports sustainable growth. Compensation plans should be revisited regularly to confirm alignment with evolving priorities, preventing mismatches that erode strategic effectiveness. When properly designed, incentive structures become a driving force behind company success rather than an obstacle to execution.

Case Study: Losing Top Talent to a Flawed Plan

Sometimes the full impact of a poorly structured compensation plan only becomes clear in retrospect. A mid-size SaaS company redesigned its plan mid-year to prioritize gross margin over total contract value. In doing so, it eliminated accelerators and introduced more stringent quota requirements without adjusting for the tougher economic climate or reduced inbound leads. The plan was rolled out with minimal sales teams input and no territory realignment, even though market dynamics had shifted significantly. Within two quarters, the company's top salespeople—who had consistently exceeded quota in prior years— were missing targets, frustrated by the lack of control, and earning less. Several left for competitors. While the plan had good intentions, the rollout ignored critical variables like rep morale, external conditions, and fairness.

Real-Life Example: One of the company's highest-earning salesperson, saw his OTE drop by 40% despite putting in the same level of effort as always before. In an exit interview, he cited a "lack of transparency and reward predictability" as the final reason for his departure. He moved to a competitor and brought two key accounts with him. The company eventually reverted to its old plan, but by then, the disruption had already cost it market share and internal credibility.

CONCLUSION

Sales compensation should never be set and forgotten. It requires constant tuning, honest feedback loops, and a clear line of sight between effort, reward, and business impact.

Mistakes in compensation design don't just cost money—they cost trust, culture, and top talent. By identifying common pitfalls early—whether it is overpaying, misaligning incentives, demotivating high performers, or failing to adapt plans with transparency—you protect both your people and your business. A well-calibrated sales compensation plan drives performance, supports strategy, and sustains success. In a competitive market, that edge can make all the difference.

Avoiding the common pitfalls is not just about fixing mistakes—it is about designing a system that consistently drives the right outcomes, attracts top talent, and reinforces your long-term strategy.

In a competitive market, alignment can be your greatest advantage.

CHAPTER 7

Analytics & Optimization

*Data-Driven Sales Compensation: Building,
Measuring, and Evolving High-Impact Incentive Plans
(How to Get Sales Compensation Analytics Right)*

A data-driven approach to Sales Compensation and Performance Management drives smarter business decisions and improved outcomes.

> But what exactly should companies measure? And how do you use those insights to build better, more adaptive compensation plans?

Problem: Without robust analytics, companies operate blind. They don't know if their compensation plans are effective—or quietly damaging performance, margins, and morale.

Result: Leveraging data-driven insights allows you to **refine, validate, and optimize** compensation structures continuously, driving sustainable growth and profitability.

- ▸ The Cost of Guesswork: When Compensation Goes Wrong
- ▸ Key Metrics: Understanding the Pulse of Your Compensation Plan
- ▸ Performance Analysis: Getting Below the Surface.
- ▸ Designing for Flexibility: How to Future-Proof Your Plan.
- ▸ Continuous Feedback Loops: Iteration as Strategy.
- ▸ Aligning Compensation with Customer Experience.
- ▸ The Role of Sales Leadership in Compensation Success.

Real-World Insight: How RevOps Drove Better Deal Quality.

Learnings: After reading this chapter, you will be able to identify and pre-emptively avoid the most common pitfalls in sales compensation design. You will develop a strategic framework to correct course when problems arise and gain a deep understanding of why compensation planning must be grounded in rigorous modelling and continuous testing. Whether you're launching a new sales team, refining a legacy plan, or scaling rapidly, this chapter will help you embrace Sales Compensation as a dynamic business strategy, not a static spreadsheet exercise.

Sales compensation as a living system. Too often, sales compensation is treated as a one-and-done initiative. A plan is rolled out at the start of the fiscal year and, barring a major failure, is rarely revisited until it is time to draft next year's version. This static approach ignores the fluid nature of business itself. Markets change. Buyer behaviours shift. Competitors introduce new offers. Products evolve. As such, sales compensation must function as a living system, one that reflects the changing dynamics of your business.

There is an importance of a data-driven sales compensation strategy. Sales compensation is often mistakenly approached as a system that can be configured once and left alone. However, to truly fuel sustainable performance, a sales compensation plan must evolve in tandem with the business and often also the economy. This means that measurement, analysis, and iteration must be embedded into the very fabric of your approach. A data-driven strategy not only offers fairness and transparency but also provides the diagnostic power necessary to spot inefficiencies, identify trends, and adapt quickly to market or internal changes.

When companies embrace a data-driven feedback loop, they position themselves to make smarter, faster, and more strategic decisions. They can isolate successful behaviours, root out inefficiencies, and fine-tune the system in real time. This leads to a tighter alignment between sales execution and business strategy, improved morale among sales teams, and a higher return on compensation spend.

Too often, organizations fall back on outdated models or assumptions, using legacy plans that no longer align with modern sales dynamics. Question the: 'We have always done it that way' approach. Decisions are made based on instinct or anecdotal evidence, which leaves sales leaders blind to the real issues undermining performance. Without robust data, it becomes impossible to determine if salespeople are being compensated fairly, if incentives are reinforcing the right behaviours, or if underperformance stems from flaws in the compensation design itself. For instance, if you are unclear about your actual Cost of Goods Sold (COGS) or the true profit margins across your product portfolio, you may inadvertently be rewarding sales that are unprofitable leading to wasted resources, demoralized teams, and missed growth targets.

To build a resilient and effective sales compensation strategy, companies need to embed analysis and optimization into their operational cadence. This means not only reviewing outcomes after (at least) a quarter but using real-time feedback to spot issues as they emerge. When treated as a dynamic engine, compensation becomes a lever for continuous improvement rather than a source of annual friction.

A data-driven approach to compensation empowers companies to move away from guesswork and legacy assumptions. Instead of relying on anecdotal success stories or outdated industry benchmarks, leaders can base decisions on empirical evidence. This results in a plan that is more aligned, fair, and motivating—and ultimately, more profitable.

The Cost of Guesswork: When Compensation Goes Wrong

Sales leaders sometimes underestimate the cost of a misaligned compensation plan. A flawed plan doesn't just affect commission payouts; it distorts behaviour, undermines morale, and erodes trust. If sales reps feel that their effort isn't being rewarded fairly—or worse, that the system is rewarding gaming or politics over true performance—they will disengage.

This erosion of trust can ripple across the organization, impacting collaboration between departments and reducing confidence in leadership decisions.

Compensation misalignment can also lead to significant financial waste. Paying above-market rates for low-margin business or rewarding volume without regard for profitability can rapidly eat into company margins. Moreover, without clear visibility into metrics like Cost of Goods Sold COGS, margin by product, or customer acquisition cost, it becomes impossible to determine whether commissions are truly earning a return.

Some of the most common pitfalls in sales compensation include:

▶ Overcomplicating the plan with too many variables
▶ Misaligning incentives with business priorities (e.g., rewarding bookings over revenue recognition)
▶ Ignoring territory disparities that create uneven opportunity
▶ Failing to account for different sales motions (e.g., new business vs. upsell vs. renewals)

THE COST OF GUESSWORK

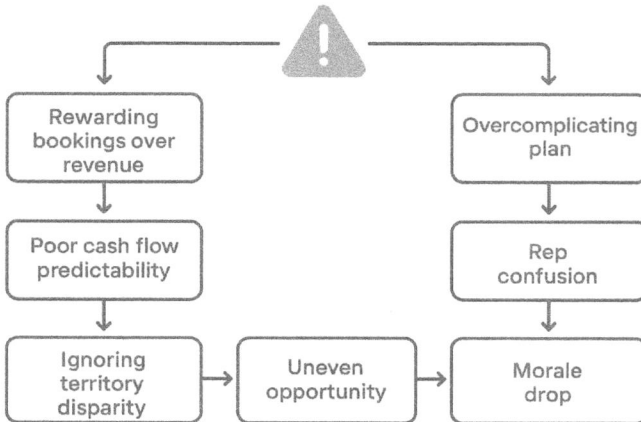

Recognizing these warning signs early is critical. With the right data, companies can identify root causes and course-correct before problems escalate.

Key Metrics: Understanding the Pulse of Your Compensation Plan

To evaluate whether your sales compensation model is functioning as intended, you must track a set of strategic performance metrics. These metrics act as the dashboard of your plan's overall health. One essential indicator is the Cost of Sales—a measure of how much you are spending in variable compensation to generate each dollar of revenue. If this figure is climbing faster than revenue, it may be a signal that your incentive structure is too rich or misaligned.

Another vital metric is Commission Efficiency, which looks at whether your salespeople are being rewarded in direct proportion to the value they create. If top performers are losing low-margin or highly discounted deals just to hit volume targets, it may suggest that incentives are driving the wrong behaviour. This dovetails with Margin Impact, which examines whether your sales compensation plan is steering salespeople toward profitable business or merely rewarding volume at any cost.

Payback Period is also critical. This tells you how long it takes to recoup your customer acquisition costs—including commissions and bonuses. A longer payback period may be acceptable for high-lifetime-value customers but should raise flags for lower-value, high-churn segments. Understanding these dynamics allows you to calibrate your plan to encourage deals that support long-term business health.

Incorporating a rolling average of these metrics over time can reveal trendlines and prevent overreacting to temporary fluctuations.

There are many more effective indicators to check on regularly.

▶ **Cost of Sales –** This part measures how much you spend to generate each dollar of revenue. If compensation costs are rising disproportionately compared to sales growth, it could indicate an unscalable model. Tracking this metric helps ensure that your investment in sales talent is yielding a positive ROI.
▶ **Commission Efficiency –** Are sales representatives being rewarded in proportion to the profit and value they generate? If

high payouts are going to deals that require deep discounts or long implementation cycles, your plan might be incentivizing inefficient behaviour.

▸ **Payback Period** – How quickly do customer acquisition costs (including commissions) get recouped? This represents the time it takes to recover the cost of customer acquisition, including commissions and bonuses. A long payback period may be acceptable in high-growth startups, but as a company matures, tightening this window becomes a sign of operational maturity.

▸ **Margin Impact** – Are incentives encouraging profitable deals, or just revenue volume? Sales teams that are rewarded solely based on top-line revenue may prioritize closing deals at any cost. By incorporating margin thresholds or profitability gates into your compensation plan, you ensure sales reps are closing high-quality deals that align with financial goals.

KEY METRICS DASHBOARD MOCKUP

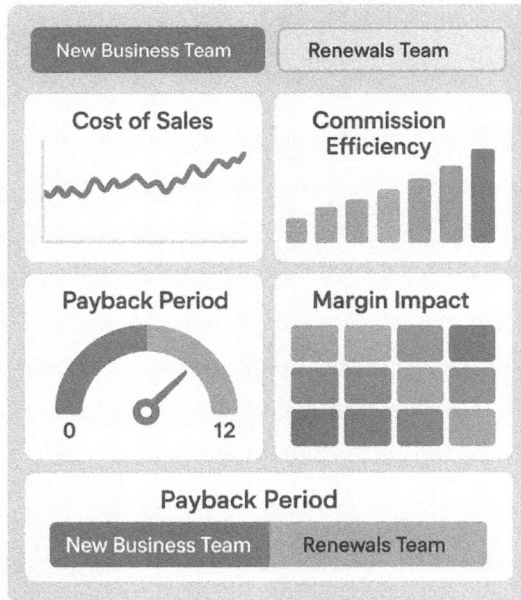

New Business Team	Renewals Team
Cost of Sales	Commission Efficiency
Payback Period	Margin Impact

Payback Period

| New Business Team | Renewals Team |

These metrics help determine whether your plan is sustainable and aligned with financial objectives. Combining these metrics into a real-time dashboard allows leadership to quickly identify trends, inefficiencies, and opportunities for plan optimization.

Performance Analysis: Getting Below the Surface

Raw performance numbers can be deceiving if not contextualized properly. On paper, a salesperson may appear to be underperforming, but a deeper analysis might reveal that they're working in an under-served or highly competitive territory. Conversely, a high-performing salesperson might be benefiting disproportionately from an easier segment or a more lucrative client list.

It is vital to see beyond the numbers and understand sales representatives performance in context.

Advanced analytics allow organizations to distinguish between effort and outcome. By analysing quota attainment, pipeline coverage, deal cycle length, and conversion rates alongside contextual variables like territory potential and lead quality, you can start to identify the root causes of performance variance. Layering in manager feedback and CRM activity data further enriches this picture, revealing effort that raw results might obscure. This level of insight is crucial not just for compensation fairness, but also for coaching, team development, and territory planning. It ensures that recognition, rewards, and developmental feedback are all grounded in reality—not just perceptions.

While data is essential, numbers don't tell the whole story. Purely quantitative assessments—like quota attainment or revenue closed—must be interpreted in context. Not all sales reps are playing on a level field. One might have a high-performing territory with strong inbound leads, while another is building a new region from scratch.

Advanced performance analysis digs deeper into pipeline health, activity levels, win rates, and average deal size, while also factoring in qualitative data from front-line managers. Are sales reps putting in the effort but not seeing results due to a flawed plan, or is it a coaching and enablement issue? This layered view helps companies avoid punishing high-effort sales reps and over-rewarding those benefiting from favourable conditions.

Moreover, understanding performance in context is critical for career development and retention. High-potential reps may leave if they feel their growth is being stifled by poor plan design or lack of recognition. Data-informed insights support more tailored coaching, smarter territory planning, and more equitable rewards.

PERFORMANCE ANALYSIS

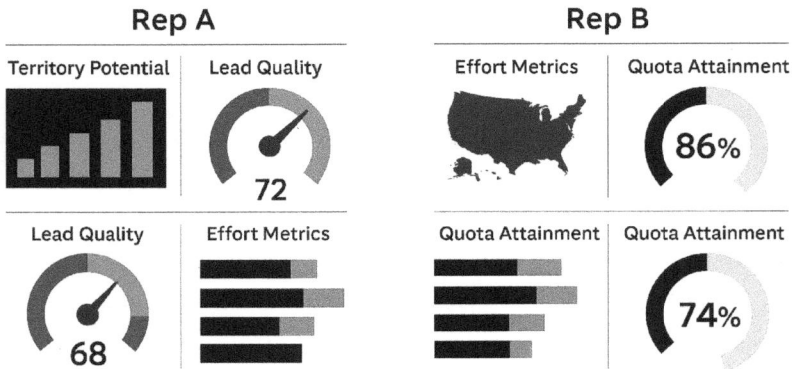

Designing for Flexibility: How to Future-Proof Your Plan

A modern sales compensation plan must be designed with adaptability in mind. Business models evolve, especially in today's fast-moving environments. New products launch. Revenue targets shift. Strategic priorities change. Compensation plans need to be able to flex accordingly.

This doesn't mean rewriting the entire plan every quarter—but it does mean building in mechanisms for regular review and iterative change. For example, companies might use quarterly SPIFFs (Sales Performance Incentive Funds) to temporarily promote behaviours that support short-term goals, such as accelerating adoption of a new feature or entering a new vertical.

Other techniques include using performance tiers, pay-mix flexibility, and "guardrail clauses"—automated limits that prevent excessive pay-outs on non-profitable deals.

Flexibility also means preparing sales compensation plans to scale with business complexity, such as introducing multi-role structures (e.g., SDRs, AEs, CSMs) or international teams.

The key is to treat compensation design not as a rigid formula, but as a strategy toolbox—one that you can adapt and deploy based on evolving needs.

Continuous Feedback Loops: Iteration as Strategy

Sales compensation in reality should be treated as a living strategy. The most successful companies do not treat sales compensation as a 'one-time' or 'once a year' project instead, they operate on a feedback cycle of **test → measure → learn → optimize**.

After each sales period, gather data not just on results but on sales behaviour. Did sales representatives chase the right deals? Did the plan encourage gaming? What feedback is coming from the front lines?

Incorporating sentiment surveys, team huddles, and A/B testing of incentive structures can rapidly surface small friction points before they become systemic problems.

Iteration doesn't always mean major change. Sometimes it is a subtle tweak—a new threshold, a revised payout curve, or a clearer definition of qualifying revenue. Over time, these small adjustments compound into a plan that is smarter, more motivating, and more aligned with growth.

Aligning Compensation with Customer Experience

An often-overlooked aspect of sales compensation is its impact on customer experience. If salespeople are rewarded purely for closing deals—without regard for implementation quality, customer fit, or retention risk—companies may see short-term wins but long-term churn.

Leading organizations now include customer retention metrics, such as NPS or net revenue retention, in sales compensation structures. This alignment often involves shared goals between Sales and Success teams, creating a hand-off that feels seamless to the customer. By tying part of the compensation to downstream outcomes, you reduce short-sighted behaviour and increase deal quality.

Moreover, this approach fosters greater alignment across go-to-market teams. When Sales, Marketing, and Customer Success all work toward shared goals—and are compensated accordingly—it creates a more seamless customer journey and a healthier revenue engine.

The Role of Sales Leadership in Compensation Success

No compensation plan succeeds in isolation. Sales leaders play a critical role in ensuring that the strategy is well-understood, embraced, and effectively executed. This requires more than just explaining the mechanics of the plan—it means reinforcing the behaviours the plan is designed to encourage.

Leaders must model transparency, continuously communicating how compensation aligns with company goals. They should also advocate for their teams, providing feedback to RevOps and Finance when plan elements create friction or confusion. Most importantly, they must coach salespeople not just to earn commissions, but to maximize impact in line with strategic priorities.

By making sales compensation a regular topic of one-on-ones, team meetings, and quarterly business reviews, sales leaders can reinforce its importance and drive accountability. When salespeople see that leadership is invested in the plan's fairness and effectiveness, it builds trust—and that trust is a powerful motivator.

Real-World Insight: How RevOps Drove Better Deal Quality

Let us take a closer look at a real-world example. A mid-sized B2B SaaS company was scaling rapidly, adding sales reps across multiple regions. Despite strong top-line growth, leadership was concerned about shrinking margins. A new RevOps leader introduced a comprehensive real-time compensation dashboard, tracking deal-level profitability, discount rates, and individual salespeople performance.

Within two quarters, the dashboard revealed that sales reps were frequently discounting deals just to hit quota. The compensation plan prioritized volume and failed to account for deal quality. As a result, sales reps were closing low-margin business that met short-term targets but harmed long-term profitability.

In response, the RevOps team redesigned the compensation structure. They introduced a profitability modifier that increased commission for high margin deals and reduced it for heavily discounted ones. They also included a lifetime value (LTV) bonus for deals expected to yield multi-year contracts.

By pairing these structural changes with transparent explanation and real-time dashboards, the company kept salespeople engaged and motivated throughout the transition.

The result? Within three months, discounting dropped by 18%, average deal size grew by 12%, and overall margins improved without hurting conversion rates.

CONCLUSION

Compensation as Strategic Infrastructure

Sales compensation is more than a pay mechanism. It is a strategic infrastructure that shapes behaviour, reflects priorities, and drives results. When built on a foundation of data, context, and continuous iteration, compensation becomes one of the most powerful tools in your growth arsenal.

Pro Tip: Hire a skilled business analyst who thrives on finding signal in the noise. The ability to turn sales data into insight—and insight into better sales compensation decisions—is priceless. Someone who can read and understand data!

Rather than fearing complexity, companies should embrace the nuances of compensation design. With the right systems, insights, and leadership alignment, sales compensation can evolve from a necessary cost centre into a competitive advantage—one that motivates teams, supports scalable growth, and strengthens the bottom line.

CHAPTER 8

Implementation & Communication

Implementing & Communicating Sales Compensation Plans

Even the most well-designed sales compensation plan will fall short if it is not implemented properly and clearly communicated to everyone involved.

What are best practices for successfully rolling out and communicating a new sales compensation plan?

Problem: Even the strongest sales compensation plan can fail without clear communication and execution, leading to confusion, misalignment, and frustration.

Result: A well-structured rollout and communication strategy ensure buy-in from sales teams, leadership and all on a 'need to know' basis, maximizing adoption and impact. Sales compensation should be an integral part of your company's training plan!

- ▸ Why Great Plans Still Fail.
- ▸ Implementation as a Strategic Inflection Point.
- ▸ Aligning Internally: Building a Cross-Functional Foundation.
- ▸ Communicating with Sales Teams: More Than Just the What.
- ▸ Training and Enablement: Turning Understanding Into Action.
- ▸ Creating Feedback Loops & Handling Disputes.
- ▸ Keeping the Plan Alive.

Real-Life Example: The "Compensation Academy" Model.

Learnings: This chapter is not about designing the plan—it is about ensuring the plan lives, breathes, and delivers results through strategic rollout and clear communication. We will explore why compensation plans often fail at the point of delivery, how to avoid the most common pitfalls, and how to build a repeatable implementation playbook that gets people on board—especially those on the front lines.

Even the most carefully designed sales compensation plan can fail if it is not implemented with precision and communicated clearly. Even the most effective sales compensation plan that took you months of careful planning, data modelling, stakeholder negotiation, and refinement—if this plan is not implemented well, it might as well not exist. Poor execution and unclear communication can sink even the most thoughtfully designed structure, eroding trust, misaligning behaviours, and ultimately, impacting revenue by creating downstream challenges for pipeline forecasting and territory management. Reasons for unsuccessful sales plans could bet: the lack of cross-functional alignment, confusing messaging, or insufficient training of those that should be involved, including the sales teams.

Success is not just about the figures on paper—it is about the clarity, transparency, and trust established throughout the rollout. For sales teams to fully engage, they need to grasp not only **what** the plan entails, but **why** it exists and **how** it supports their goals. Without that understanding, confusion sets in, alignment is lost, and motivation quickly fades. And they are not the only people that need to understand the thought process behind the plan design. Everyone in the organization that is maintaining the plan or executing on any of the elements needs to be informed as well. Ideally you are maintaining a list of people on a 'need to know' basis. Use methods like a RACI matrix* (see footnote), DACI, Gantt or any other.

It is not uncommon for companies to invest months designing a great sales compensation plan, only to rush through rollout or skip stakeholder alignment. The result? Salespeople don't fully understand how they are paid, finance teams are raising red flags, and disputes multiply. Poor communication leads to mistrust and misalignment, even if the plan itself is solid.

A thoughtful rollout backed by clear, consistent communication fosters trust, drives adoption, and ensures everyone—from frontline sales reps to senior leadership—is aligned. When compensation plans are explained well and sales reps can see how the structure supports their success, they are far more likely to engage, commit, and perform. Implementation isn't just a step—it is a strategic moment that shapes perception and performance.

Footnote: *A RACI matrix is a responsibility assignment chart used in project management to clarify roles and responsibilities for each task within a project or process. **RACI** stands for **Responsible, Accountable, Consulted, and Informed**. It visually represents who is responsible for doing the work, who is ultimately accountable for its completion, who needs to be consulted for input, and who needs to be informed of progress. **DACI** is something vagally comparable and stands for **Driver, Approver, Contributor, Informed**.*

Why Great Plans Still Fail

Sales compensation plans often unravel not in the boardroom, but on the sales floor. The challenge isn't just in the mechanics of calculating commission or quotas—it is in how those mechanics are received, understood, and believed.

Imagine investing months perfecting a plan that aligns flawlessly with company strategy. It is tied to customer retention, growth in new verticals, and expansion of long-term contracts. On paper, it is everything the business needs. But it is rolled out via a dense PDF on a Friday afternoon, with no walkthrough, no examples, no narrative, and no forum for questions. Monday morning, the sales team is confused. By Wednesday, they are speculating in Slack (Here: The cloud-based team communication platform owned by Salesforce since 2020). By Friday, someone files a complaint with HR.

Kick-offs are powerful for high-level storytelling and emotional momentum—but they must be followed by structured enablement and ongoing clarification.

This scenario is not fiction—it happens frequently, and it is costly. Poor implementation creates suspicion, and suspicion kills motivation. If a sales representative doesn't trust the compensation plan—or worse, doesn't understand it—they are not selling at full capacity. They are distracted, cautious, and likely to default to the safest, least innovative selling behaviour. And leadership often misinterprets that caution as resistance or poor performance.

If your sales team doesn't understand what they asked to do, they use their own interpretation and may unintentionally undermine key business priorities. Not only that, but they will also go after what is the easiest in reach for them and not what you have designed them to do.

Implementation as a Strategic Inflection Point

Rolling out a sales compensation plan isn't an operational detail—it is a moment of cultural significance. It is the point where a company's **strategy meets its people**. If executed thoughtfully, this moment becomes a launchpad for clarity, momentum, and unity. If neglected, it becomes a breeding ground for confusion, disengagement, and attrition. This moment determines whether salespeople see the company's goals as aligned with their own—or as imposed from above.

When implementation is viewed as an afterthought, the organization sends a signal: "This plan isn't important enough to warrant explanation." But when it is treated as a strategic priority, the message is clear: "We are invested in your success, and this plan is a key part of it."

A thoughtful implementation strategy aligns all departments, empowers managers, equips salespeople, and closes the distance between corporate vision and individual action.

Aligning Internally: Building a Cross-Functional Foundation

Before a single slide is shown to the sales team, the internal groundwork must be in place. Implementation starts with alignment, particularly across Sales, Finance, Rev/-or Sales/Ops, HR, and Executive Leadership. If even one of these functions is misaligned—or worse, uninformed—the entire rollout is at risk.

Sales may focus on drive and motivation. Finance is tuned into cost control, forecasting, and fiscal responsibility. HR is concerned with compliance, fairness, and communication. Executives want results, predictability, and accountability. Meanwhile, RevOps or Sales Ops plays a central role in orchestrating the end-to-end process—translating strategic goals into operational reality, aligning systems and data, modelling scenarios, and ensuring that plan mechanics actually function as intended. Each of these stakeholders looks at compensation through a different lens, but all are essential.

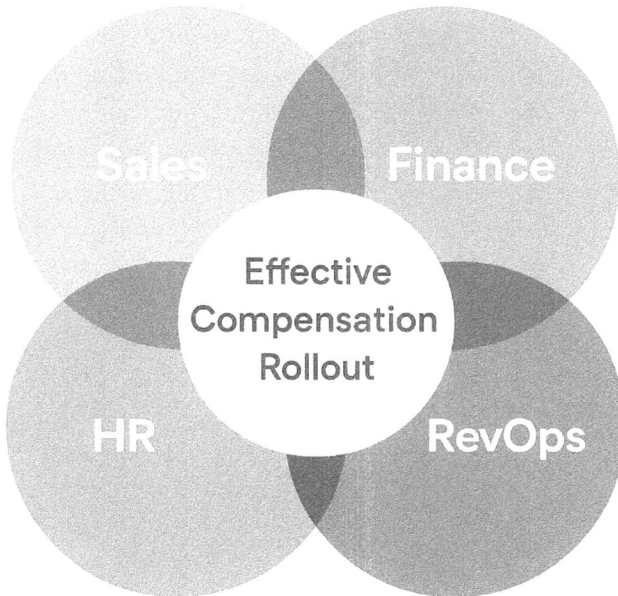

One of the first levels to be aligned with, is your **Leadership** level. **Get Executive Buy-In!**

Gaining early executive sponsorship is critical. The best implementation teams don't just ask for approval—they **build advocacy**. This means presenting the plan not just as a set of numbers, but as a story that supports strategic objectives. Why are we shifting incentives toward multi-year deals? How does this align with our long-term valuation goals? Why reduce accelerators for low-margin product lines? Frame these decisions as strategic levers, not just compensation tweaks.

Executives who believe in the rationale will echo it in town halls, performance reviews, and board meetings. They become cultural amplifiers, reinforcing the "why" behind the "what." Their buy-in also protects the compensation plan during turbulent quarters, when pressure to 'adjust on the fly' can derail consistency.

Next on your list is **Finance & HR!**

Finance must be confident the plan is financially sustainable, and HR needs to confirm it is legally compliant and ethically sound. Involve both early. Bring them into modelling sessions. Invite them to challenge assumptions. Doing so builds trust and reduces the risk of last-minute objections that could derail the rollout. In some countries you will also need to harmonize the sales compensation plan with workers-council or union. Allow enough time for that!

Example: At a mid-sized SaaS company, a Sales VP worked closely with Finance to simulate the cost of a new variable pay structure across low-, mid-, and high-performing sales representatives. When rolled out, the CFO personally addressed the team, explaining how the structure supported company health. The sales representatives took notice—not just of the numbers, but of the alignment between departments.

Communicating with Sales Teams: More Than Just the What

Once internal alignment is achieved, it is time to turn outward—to the people who will live with the plan day-to-day. Sales representatives don't just need a PDF; they need narrative, examples, interaction, and clarity. Ideally you also make interactive tools such as compensation calculators, FAQs, and peer-led learning sessions available.

Telling the Story Behind the Plan

Every compensation plan has a story. Maybe it is about entering new markets. Maybe it is about rewarding land-and-expand strategies. Maybe it is about shifting from product sales to customer success.

Don't hide that story—lead with it. Salespeople are far more receptive when they see the logic behind the structure. And it fosters respect when leadership explains, candidly, why certain elements exist—even if they are tough changes. Be open about the strategy that is the fundament of the plan design.

Example: One B2B hardware company needed to reduce commissions on legacy products that were declining in profitability. Rather than bury the change in a table, leadership opened with the financial reality: shrinking margins were putting pressure on other parts of the business. Then, they showed how salespeople could earn even more by shifting focus to bundled solutions. Framing it as a growth strategy, not a penalty, shifted perception.

Making It Real: Simulations and Examples

One of the most effective tools in communication is the earnings simulation. Walk salespeople through different scenarios: a top performer, a mid-level achiever, and someone struggling. Show exactly what the payout would look like under the new plan. Make it tangible. Visual tools like dashboards, calculators, and live modeling sessions can turn abstract rules into concrete expectations. Pair this with real-world examples: "If you close a $50K annual contract in Q1, and upsell it by $20K in Q3, here is exactly what you will earn and why." Another effective way to present the new sales compensation plan to your sales team is by showing how their payouts would have differed if the plan had been in place the previous year.

Payout Simulation

Old vs. New Plan for Sample Rep Profile

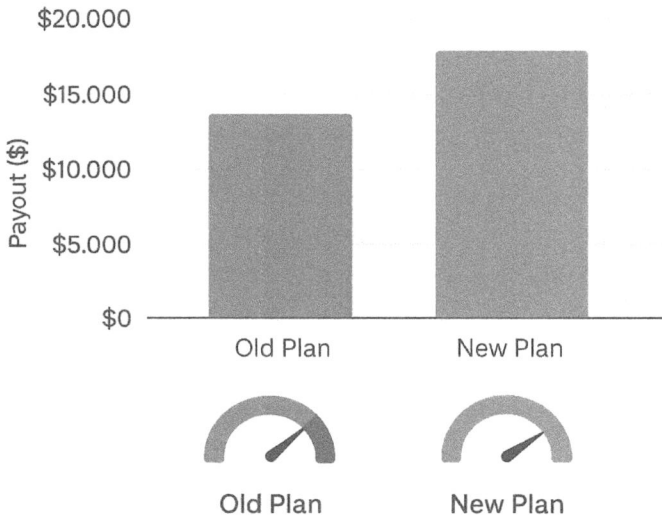

Creating Feedback Loops & Handling Disputes

Rolling out the plan isn't the end—it is the midpoint of a conversation. Questions, disputes, and misunderstandings will surface. The difference between success and frustration lies in how the organization responds. Think of it less as a finish line, and more as the opening act in a year-long performance.

Create structured channels for feedback: Q&A sessions, dedicated office hours, a shared Slack channel, or a comp-plan hotline. Ensure there is documentation available—not just for legal reasons, but for consistency and fairness. Offer 1:1 sessions in case someone in your sales team does not feel comfortable asking questions in front of everyone else. Also do refresher sessions to pick up new starters and internal transfers.

Sales representatives talk. If one person feels short-changed, others will hear about it. Proactively address issues with transparency and speed. The goal isn't to avoid questions—it is to meet them with openness and respect.

Handling Disputes

Disputes will happen, and how they are handled determines whether your culture grows stronger or weaker. The key is to approach every concern with transparency, consistency, and a mindset of continuous improvement—especially for global teams with varying local expectations. Resist the urge to get defensive. Instead, treat each complaint as a valuable signal: it could highlight an area where the plan needs clearer communication or expose a flaw to be addressed in next year's design.

Establish a clear, documented dispute resolution process ahead of time. This should include a simple flowchart outlining key steps: how you want your sales team to submit concerns, who reviews them, what data is required, and which roles (e.g., Sales, RevOps, Finance) are involved at each stage. Define decision-making authority and escalation paths so that disputes don't stall or escalate unnecessarily. Store all related documentation securely and ensure it is accessible to the right teams—typically within RevOps or HR.

Example: Suppose a salesperson believes their Q1 payout is $5,000 short due to a territory crediting issue. With a structured process in place, they submit a formal query through a standard form. A designated liaison from RevOps or Sales Operations—someone neutral and removed from direct performance conversations—reviews the CRM and compensation system data, consults with Sales Ops and Finance, and provides a fact-based response. This approach prevents finger-pointing and preserves the relationship between the salespeople and their manager.

Finally, be mindful of precedent. If you make an exception, recognize that others may expect similar treatment. Consistency is key to maintaining fairness—and credibility—in your compensation plan.

Training and Enablement: Turning Understanding Into Action

Implementation isn't just communication—it is enablement. Salespeople don't just need to hear the plan, they need to internalize it, remember it, and apply it to real decisions.

Training as a Strategic Lever

Too often, training is treated as an afterthought—a quick webinar or an email with a slide deck. But compensation training should be integrated into your overall sales enablement strategy.

Think of it as onboarding, even for existing salespeople. Include sessions on:

- ▶ How to read a compensation plan
- ▶ How to track performance during the month, quarter, half-year and year
- ▶ How variable pay ties into OTE (On Target Earnings)

What happens in edge cases (deal splits, customer churn, etc.)

Incorporate role-playing or mini-case studies. Give managers toolkits for coaching. Provide ongoing access to reference material—not just at rollout, but throughout the year.

Keeping the Plan Alive

Even the best-implemented plan can fade into the background if it is not revisited. Implementation is not a one-time event—it is the beginning of an annual rhythm.

Quarterly reviews help remind salespeople of how the plan works, what behaviours are being rewarded, and how strategy may be evolving. These reviews also serve as a barometer: is the plan still driving the right behaviours? Are incentives still aligned?

Use these touchpoints to gather insight, surface patterns, and build a library of case studies that inform future iterations.

Real-World Example: The "Compensation Academy" Model

A global enterprise software company created an internal "Compensation Academy" to support plan rollouts. It included a self-paced eLearning module, interactive earnings simulations tailored to each sales rep's region and role, and a mandatory quiz to confirm comprehension.

Managers held follow-up sessions with small teams to discuss personal questions. At the end of the first quarter, a feedback survey captured insights and confusion points, which fed into version 2.0 of the training.

The result? Salespeople reported significantly higher satisfaction with their compensation structure, and plan adoption was near total. But the real win was cultural: the initiative signalled that the company took their compensation—and their success—seriously.

An additional result was that the outcome of the quiz influenced the design of the sales compensation plan for the following year.

CONCLUSION

Implementation as a Cultural Signal

Sales compensation is more than a financial model. It is a reflection of what a company values, where it is headed, and how it plans to get there. When you implement a plan with care, communicate it with clarity, and support it with ongoing conversation, you are not just launching a pay structure—you are building trust, transparency, and shared ambition.

In many ways, how you roll out a plan matters just as much as what the plan says. This chapter isn't just a how-to—it is a call to treat implementation as a moment of alignment, storytelling, and leadership. When done right, it doesn't just clarify goals. It energizes your team to go out and achieve the goals.

When salespeople feel informed, involved, and respected, they don't just follow a plan—they champion it!

CHAPTER 9

SPIF's and Other Incentive Drivers

Using SPIF's and other Rewards to drive the right behaviour
Leveraging other drivers to fine-tune outcome like special incentives

While cash remains a core motivator, sales reps are often driven by more nuanced rewards that can significantly enhance performance. When standard compensation structures lack urgency or fail to direct attention to specific goals, special incentives like SPIFs become essential performance levers. These additional levers allow organizations to influence outcomes in a timely, tactical way without overhauling the broader compensation strategy.

> **What options are there to fine-tune outcome and behaviour during a financial year and address special situations?**

Problem: Traditional compensation plans often lack the immediacy or precision needed to drive short-term focus, resulting in missed tactical opportunities.

Solution: Special incentives like SPIFs offer timely, focused motivation—delivering performance exactly where and when it matters most.

- ▸ What are SPIF's, when to use them and how to set them up.
- ▸ How to use internal competitions effectively to drive growth.
- ▸ Why a President's Club is still current.
- ▸ Non-cash Incentives: When recognition outweighs rewards.

Real-World Example: How a company successfully used incentives outside of the regular plan design.

Learnings: After reading this chapter you will be empowered to fine-tune performance and drive strategic outcomes beyond the limitations of standard compensation plans. By exploring the targeted use of SPIFs, short-term contests, and recognition programs like President's Club, this chapter aims to show how to create urgency, boost engagement, and reinforce high-performance culture. This chapter is designed to help organizations deploy incentives that not only energize sales teams but also align with broader business objectives—without compromising structural consistency. Ultimately, the goal is to provide the tools and thinking needed to make short-term incentives both impactful and sustainable through clear design, transparent measurement, and purposeful communication.

Sales reps are motivated by more than just cash — although cash is one of the main drivers. In addition, there are strategic rewards that can significantly enhance motivation and drive performance. To fine-tune outcomes during the financial year, you can leverage special incentives such as SPIFs or internal competitions.

What are SPIFs, when to use them, and how to set them up:

A SPIF (**S**ales **P**erformance **I**ncentive **F**und)—also known as a SPIFF—is a powerful short-term incentive designed to create immediate impact without altering your base compensation plan. Think of it as a "booster rocket" that ignites when you need quick acceleration toward specific goals.

67% of companies use SPIFs to motivate their Sales Teams to:

- ▶ Accelerate new products into the market.
- ▶ Accelerate growth into new territories.
- ▶ Increase sales for high margin products.
- ▶ Speed up implementation.
- ▶ Improve customer satisfaction.
- ▶ Move old inventory to free up space.

▶ Build brand preference with channel partners.
▶ Give a boost to sales for a specific time period (to meet quarterly sales goals, for example).

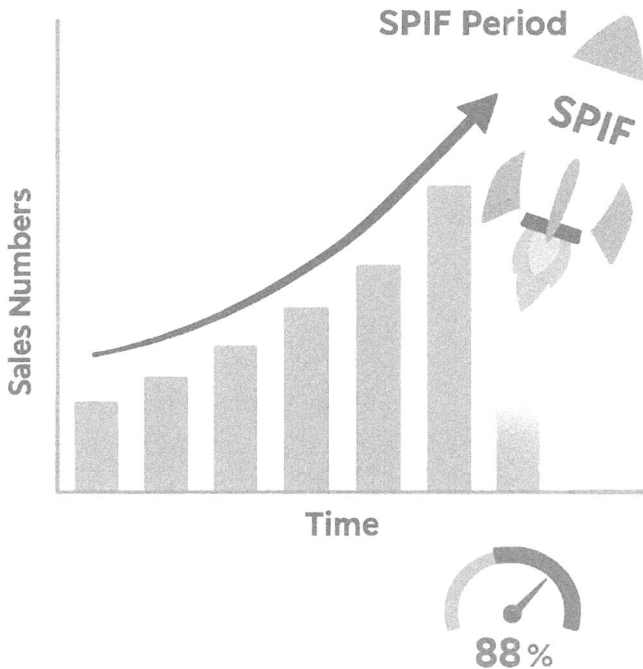

Usage Rules and Best Practices:

Important note: Avoid running too many SPIFs concurrently, as this can dilute focus, misalign with strategic priorities, and create confusion among salespeople. Use a structured SPIF template for each initiative, with clearly defined rules. Always conduct a post-campaign analysis to measure effectiveness and identify improvements. Do an analysis after, to see how successful your SPIF has been. Be mindful of creating SPIF dependency—salespeople should not delay strategic selling in anticipation of the next special incentive. Repeating SPIFs does not make them special anymore and the sales teams are expecting them when repeated regularly.

Top Tip: Always set clear eligibility criteria, communication cadence, and payout timelines. A **SPIF Template** should include:

- Target behaviour.
- Eligible sales reps or channels.
- Timeframe.
- Payout conditions.
- Measurement method.
- Budget cap.
- Review/analysis section.

You will find a draft SPIF template in the Appendix.

Real-Life Example: A SaaS company launched a new analytics module mid-year. Despite training and enablement efforts, uptake was slow. A 45-day SPIF gave sales reps a $500 bonus for each closed deal including the new module. Result? 63% of eligible sales reps sold the module during the SPIF window and attach rate rose from 8% to 28%—far exceeding initial projections.

Using Internal Competitions to Drive Growth

Salespeople are naturally competitive. They thrive in environments where performance is not only rewarded, but visible. Creating internal competitions taps into this instinct and can turn an average quarter into a record-breaking one.

Salespeople are often wired to compete—not just to close deals, but to outperform their peers. To use this competitiveness and add a little fun you can add a leaderboard.

Gamification techniques can be used here effectively—leaderboards, tiered goals, surprise bonuses, and team-versus-team formats. The psychology of "not being last" or "beating your rival" is surprisingly powerful.

Competitions should not end with your typical leaderboard. To inject excitement, consider quarterly competitions with standout rewards. In one instance, the top performer was given the keys to a Ferrari for a weekend—an experience that energized the entire team and nearly doubled quarterly results. That was such a booster for the sales team that we nearly doubled the results for the quarter. We also had a quarter where the prize was an exciting luxury pullman train ride for two.

Real-Life Example: A medical device firm ran a "Sales Olympics" across its global offices with three categories: most deals, largest deal, and highest customer satisfaction. Weekly anonymous rankings were shared, and final standings revealed during a company-wide virtual event. Engagement spiked, and 5 of the 7 regions exceeded their quarterly targets.

Leaderboard Tip: For an extra bit of fun, make it anonymous for the first part and reveal the names a month before your quarter ends. If you are on a shorter cycle, like monthly, keep the outcome anonymous for the first 3 weeks and reveal for the last week. You will see that this will result in a big push towards your revenue goals. You should be able to easily get the ranking through your dashboards.

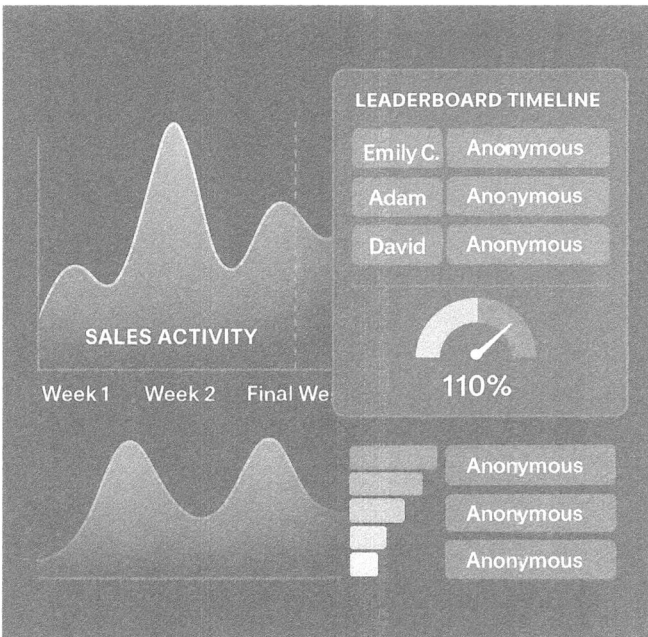

Why a President's Club Remains Relevant or Why Celebrating the successes of your Top Sales Professionals is still a good idea

In today's fast-moving, remote-enabled sales environment, some might ask: Is President's Club still relevant? The answer is a resounding **yes**, when done right.

By definition: President's Club is a prestigious award - typically involving an all-expenses-paid trip to an upscale destination - that recognizes top salespeople for highly overachieving their goals and quota. In reality, President's Club is invaluable face time with the leading Senior Executives at your company. But what is in it for the Company?

President's Club is about recognition, prestige, and aspiration. While the destination and luxury experience are appealing, the true value lies in status, exclusivity, and proximity to executive leadership. Top sales-people crave acknowledgment in front of peers, and ambitious sales reps chase this pinnacle. Other names may also be Chairman's Club, Circle of Excellence, Winner's Circle, Achiever's Club, Pinnacle, and Peak Performance Program.

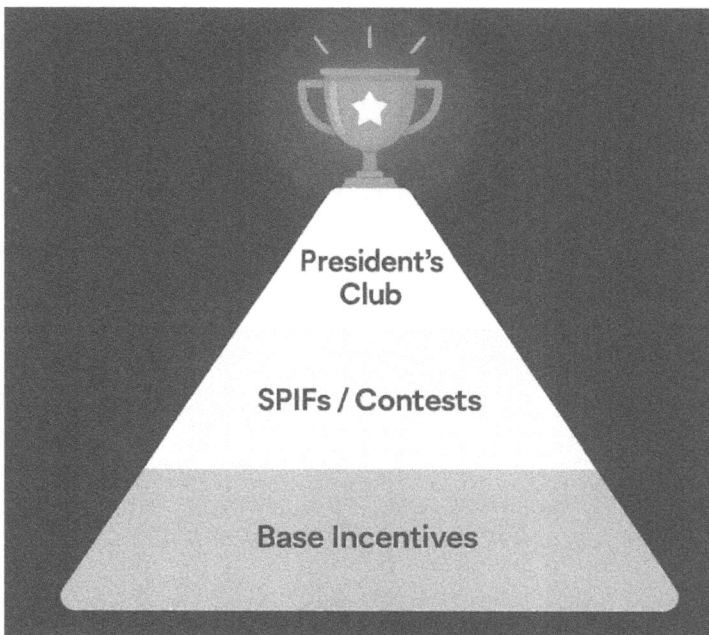

President's Club

SPIFs / Contests

Base Incentives

Real-Life Perspective: One multinational tech firm rebranded its President's Club as the "Elite Circle," focusing on peer networking, future strategy discussions with executives, and once-in-a-lifetime experiences (e.g., cooking with a celebrity chef, private island dinner, bring your partner/or a friend along). Attainment tripled in the first year. It wasn't just the trip—it was the transformation of the event into an experience.

Beyond the reward, President's Club fosters a strong culture of performance and belonging. It sends a clear message: *Excellence is celebrated here.*

Another benefit: Great things like new ideas and growth potential come from this kind of access to senior leaders.

Overall, President's Club is intended to be more than a trip; it is intended to be an unparalleled experience worthy of the top producers of the best sales team in the market. The experience is intended to reward the dedication and effort of your top performers with a white glove experience intended to tantalize all of the senses and make reality for that week, seem like a fantasy.

Non-Cash Incentives: When Recognition Outweighs Rewards

Not all motivation stems from money. In fact, in many high-performing sales cultures, recognition can be just as powerful—sometimes more so—than financial incentives. While SPIFs and President's Clubs are well-established tools, the value of non-cash rewards is increasingly evident, especially among younger generations or highly collaborative teams.

Non-cash incentives can take many forms:

- Personalized thank-you messages from senior leadership.
- Spotlight recognition in team meetings or internal communications.
- Custom experiences like a dinner with the CEO, early product access, or team retreat invitations.
- Status symbols such as award trophies, certificates, or exclusive access to strategic projects.

While seemingly minor, these gestures have a lasting psychological impact—fostering intrinsic motivation, deeper engagement, and long-term loyalty.

> **Real-Life Example:** A cybersecurity company introduced a quarterly peer-nominated award called the "Sales Catalyst Award." It had no monetary prize—just a trophy, internal announcement, and a reserved lunch with the executive team. Over time, salespeople started campaigning for nominations, collaborating more, and publicly celebrating each other's achievements. Productivity increased, and employee satisfaction scores went up by 12% in two quarters.

What this shows is that recognition isn't a consolation prize—it is a strategic lever. Used properly, it creates emotional commitment and strengthens cultural alignment.

Here are some ideas for non-monetary rewards that can be just as effective, if not more so, than monetary incentives in motivating sales teams. The suggestions are based on the nature of an extrovert salesperson:

Recognition and Awards:

- ▶ Employee of the Month/Quarter/Year awards
- ▶ Top Sales Performer recognition
- ▶ Hall of Fame for consistent top performers – build your legacy!

Professional Development Opportunities:

- ▶ Sponsored attendance to industry conferences or workshops
- ▶ Subscriptions to online learning platforms or courses
- ▶ Mentorship programs with senior sales staff or industry experts

Exclusive Perks:

- ▶ VIP parking spots
- ▶ Access to executive lounges or facilities
- ▶ Flexible work hours or remote work options for top performers

Experience Rewards:

- Team outings (e.g., dinners, team-building activities)
- Adventure experiences (e.g., hot air balloon rides, escape rooms)
- Spa days or wellness retreats

Career Advancement Opportunities:

- Fast-track to leadership programs
- Opportunities to lead special projects or initiatives
- Cross-departmental training for broader skill development

Customized Gifts:

- Personalized merchandise (e.g., engraved watches, custom-made bags)
- High-quality electronics (e.g., headphones, tablets)
- Gift cards for luxury experiences (e.g., fine dining, travel)

Time Off Incentives:

- Additional vacation days
- Extended weekends
- Half-days or early dismissal privileges

Social Recognition:

- Shout-outs in company newsletters or social media
- Public recognition during team meetings or town halls
- Featured spotlights on company intranet or bulletin boards

Competitions and Challenges:

- Sales contests with attractive prizes
- Team challenges with rewards for collective achievements
- Friendly competitions between departments or teams

Personalized Rewards:

- Tailored experiences based on individual interests (e.g., cooking classes, concert tickets)

> ▸ Customized thank-you notes or letters from senior management
> ▸ Opportunities to work on projects aligned with personal passions

Charitable Contributions:

> ▸ Donations made in the name of top performers to their chosen charities
> ▸ Volunteer opportunities during work hours
> ▸ Matching donations for fundraising efforts

The success of non-monetary incentives hinges on alignment with your team's values, interests, and professional aspirations. Additionally, regularly soliciting feedback and adjusting the incentives based on what resonates most with your team can help ensure their effectiveness over time. Check tax limits with HR!

> **Top Tip:** Pair non-cash incentives with formal programs, not just ad hoc shoutouts. Structure, regularity, and visibility make the impact measurable and sustainable.

Real-World Example: Successful Use of Special Incentives

Case Study: Mid-Year Momentum Reset

A B2B logistics firm saw Q2 sales stagnate due to seasonal lulls and sales rep fatigue. Instead of waiting for trends to shift, leadership launched a dual-incentive approach:

> ▸ SPIF: An extra €300 per contract closed that included premium support services.
> ▸ Competition: A "Fast & Focused" leaderboard tracked deal size over 6 weeks, with the top 3 winning a weekend getaway.

Result?

Sales rose 31% compared to the same period the prior year. What made it work was clarity, urgency, and visibility. Salespeople didn't just want the bonus—they wanted to win.

CONCLUSION

Sales environments are dynamic—and your incentives should be too. Driving mid-year outcomes requires more than rigid compensation plans; it demands flexible, targeted, and motivating levers. With well-crafted SPIFs, engaging competitions, and prestigious recognition events, organizations can unlock agile performance levers that align with both short-term targets and long-term culture.

Done right, these tools don't just increase revenue—they build identity and inspire excellence. Top performers aren't only motivated by money—they thrive on achievement, recognition, and purpose. And it's up to leadership to give them the right stage to perform.

CHAPTER 10

Future Trends

The Future of Sales Compensation: Staying Ahead of the Curve

Sales compensation is in constant evolution—staying ahead of trends and adapting quickly is essential to maintain a competitive edge. It is not a static practice but a dynamic system that must evolve with the business landscape. As the marketplace continues to shift, driven by technological innovations, changing customer behaviours, and evolving workforce expectations, compensation strategies must evolve alongside. In this chapter, we explore where sales compensation is headed, how to navigate this transformation, and what leaders can do to future-proof their strategies.

> **What emerging trends are shaping the future of Sales compensation, and how can businesses prepare for it?**

Problem: Traditional sales compensation plans often lag behind evolving sales roles, AI-driven automation, and emerging business models.

Result: Staying ahead of emerging trends ensures your sales compensation strategy remains competitive, future-ready, and aligned with shifting performance drivers. Leveraging the latest tools, techniques and insights to stay ahead is not optional anymore, but a strategy to stay current.

- ▸ Emerging trends in sales compensation and how to keep up-to-date and informed.
- ▸ The impact of generative AI on sales roles.

- ▶ The evolution of commission structures in a data-driven world.
- ▶ Rethinking the role of the salesperson in a hybrid future.
- ▶ The expanding role of the sales manager: leader, coach, and well-being advocate.

Case Study: What leading companies are doing to stay ahead.

Learnings: After reading this chapter, you will have all the tools and insights as to why traditional sales compensation models are no longer sufficient in today's fast-evolving business landscape. You will recognize how trends such as generative AI, data-driven performance metrics, and team-based incentive structures are transforming the way organizations reward and motivate their sales teams. This chapter equips you with the knowledge to evaluate and adapt your current compensation approach, helping you design strategies that are aligned with the future of sales. Through real-world examples and case studies, you will see how leading companies are already making these shifts—and how you can begin to implement similar innovations in your own organization to stay competitive and future-ready.

In a landscape where sales roles are rapidly transforming—becoming more consultative, tech-driven, and team-based—conventional compensation plans are losing relevance. Today's sales professionals have evolved beyond order-takers and cold-callers. They now act as solution architects, data analysts, and curators of customer experience.

As AI and automation become integrated into every stage of the sales process, tasks that were once high-effort and commission-worthy may now be completed by intelligent systems. This creates a misalignment between compensation and the actual value delivered by human sales professionals.

For example, consider a software sales representative who used to spend hours qualifying leads and booking demos. With AI handling the lead scoring and scheduling, that sales rep's role shifts toward deeper consultative selling—but the commission structure might still be rewarding top-of-funnel activities.

Staying ahead is no longer optional—it is essential for relevance and re-silience. Future-ready businesses are already reshaping how they com-pensate their salesforces. They are aligning incentives with desired be-haviours—not outdated metrics. They are using data to continuously refine compensation models and applying insights from other func-tions like marketing, product, and customer success.

By staying on top of emerging trends, companies can attract top talent, boost morale, and improve retention. More importantly, they build sales teams that are agile, motivated, and equipped to perform in an unpredictable business environment.

Emerging Trends in Sales Compensation and How to Keep Up

The sales world doesn't change all at once—but it is evolving fast. Here is how some of the most impactful trends are shaping the future of compensation:

1. Subscription and Usage-Based Models: Traditional one-time sales commissions are making way for models that reward salespeople over time. This aligns better with recurring revenue businesses like SaaS, where customer retention is as important as initial sales.

2. Team-Based Compensation: With complex deals now requiring cross-functional collaboration, many organizations are adopting team bonuses or shared quotas. This encourages cooperation and prevents "lone wolf" mentalities.

3. Personalized Compensation Plans: Data and automation allow for dynamic compensation that adapts to individual performance trends, tenure, or even behavioural metrics like customer satisfaction scores.

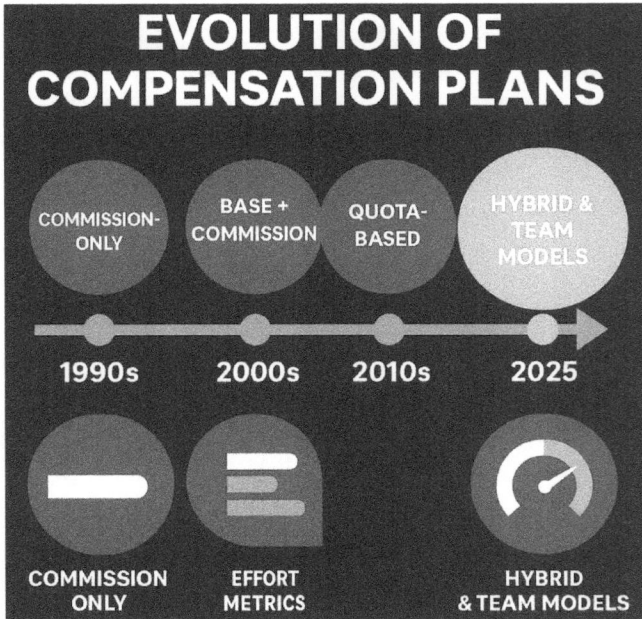

EVOLUTION OF COMPENSATION PLANS

COMMISSION-ONLY · BASE + COMMISSION · QUOTA-BASED · HYBRID & TEAM MODELS

1990s · 2000s · 2010s · 2025

COMMISSION ONLY · EFFORT METRICS · HYBRID & TEAM MODELS

4. Agile Compensation Reviews: Instead of annual reviews, forward-thinking companies are reviewing and adjusting compensation plans quarterly or even monthly based on real-time data and market dynamics.

To stay informed, leaders are investing in compensation technology, reading analyst reports (e.g., Gartner, Forrester), attending sales operations and revenue operations conferences, and experimenting through pilot programs.

The Impact of Generative AI on Sales Roles

Generative AI tools—like ChatGPT, Salesforce Einstein, Perplexity, Co-pilot and others—are fundamentally changing what a salesperson does day-to-day. These tools can write personalized emails, generate pitches, analyse deal risks, and even simulate conversations for training purposes.

As AI automates routine interactions, human salespeople are focusing more on complex problem-solving, strategic selling, and long-term relationship-building. Sales compensation plans must evolve to reward depth over volume—emphasizing strategic insight, lasting value, and meaningful engagement.

Real-life example: A multinational IT services firm introduced "AI-Aware" bonuses—rewarding salespeople who leveraged AI tools to shorten deal cycles or increase upsell conversion rates. The result: faster ramp-up times and improved win rates.

SHIFT IN SALES TIME SPENT

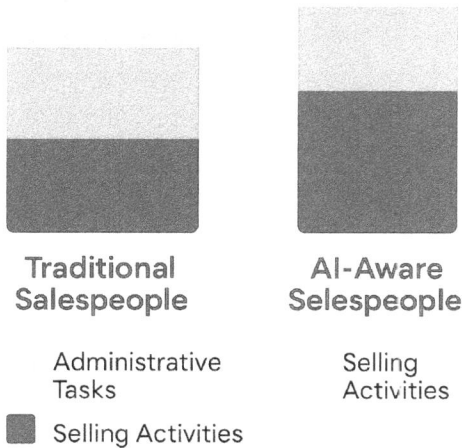

Traditional Salespeople	AI-Aware Selespeople
Administrative Tasks	Selling Activities

Selling Activities

The Evolution of Commission Structures in a Data-Driven World

Modern sales compensation is no longer just about gut feel or historical norms—it is grounded in real-time performance data, customer behaviour analytics, and predictive modelling.

Key changes include:

▸ Incentivizing lifetime value (LTV) instead of contract value alone.
▸ Using AI to identify high-ROI behaviours and tailoring rewards accordingly.
▸ Embedding non-sales metrics like Net Promoter Score (NPS) or customer engagement into compensation plans.

BONUS TRIGGERS

LTV	NPS	82
$ 120 k	70	ACTIVITY SCORE

✓ BONUS ACHIEVED

MODERN SALES DASHBOARD

Rethinking the Role of the Salesperson in a Hybrid Future

As the workplace becomes increasingly hybrid—with remote teams, asynchronous communication, and global collaboration—sales roles are evolving in both subtle and profound ways. The traditional image of the traveling salesperson or the always-on office presence is giving way to a more fluid, digitally native professional who must navigate virtual meetings, data dashboards, and AI-enhanced CRMs.

This transformation demands a new approach to performance measurement—where outcomes, not activity levels or physical presence, determine value and reward. Instead, compensation plans must be designed to recognize outcomes over optics—emphasizing the quality of customer interactions, the depth of insight provided, and the strategic value a salesperson brings to a deal.

Organizations that thrive in this hybrid future are those that foster autonomy, provide digital tools for real-time feedback and coaching, and implement compensation systems that are transparent and adaptable. For instance, progressive companies are beginning to measure "collaborative contribution" as part of performance—rewarding those who contribute to deal success across teams, even if they aren't the primary closer.

The hybrid environment also raises new questions about fairness and visibility. Remote salespeople may not have the same exposure to leadership or the same informal influence as in-office peers. Forward-looking compensation strategies can foster equity by anchoring rewards in objective data, not proximity or visibility biases.

By redefining the role of the salesperson in this modern context—and adapting compensation to fit—companies can unlock new levels of engagement, performance, and equity in their sales organizations. This is not just a tactical adjustment but a strategic advantage in attracting and retaining top talent in a competitive, increasingly distributed world.

The Expanding Role of the Sales Manager: Leader, Coach, and Well-Being Advocate

In the evolving landscape of sales organizations, the role of the sales manager has expanded far beyond hitting targets and pushing pipelines. Today's sales managers are expected not only to drive revenue but also to act as coaches, mental health advocates, and cultural leaders for their teams. This growing complexity reflects the rising importance of human-centred leadership in a high-pressure, high-performance environment.

Sales remains an emotionally demanding profession. Amid rising expectations, relentless performance tracking, and the blurred boundaries of hybrid work, salespeople face heightened risks of burnout, isolation, and disengagement. As a result, sales managers are now looked to as the first line of defence in supporting their team's mental health and work-life balance.

This responsibility introduces a new layer of leadership that many sales managers were never trained for. Managing quotas is one thing; navigating emotional fatigue, signs of burnout, or the personal challenges of remote employees is another. The skills required—empathy, emotional intelligence, active listening, and psychological safety—are now as critical as CRM fluency or sales forecasting.

To meet these demands, organizations must invest in ongoing leadership development, tailored specifically for sales managers. This includes training not only in coaching and conflict resolution, but also in wellness awareness, equitable workload distribution, and inclusive management practices. When sales managers are properly supported, they can foster healthier, more resilient teams—and better business results.

However, this shift comes at a structural cost. As the manager's responsibilities deepen, their bandwidth shrinks. The traditional span of control—typically eight to ten direct reports—has become unsustainable as emotional and developmental demands grow. With more emotional and developmental investment required per salesperson, companies are re-evaluating team sizes and creating mid-level leadership roles (such as team leads or player-coaches) to bridge the gap.

This evolution changes how sales organizations scale. It is not just about hiring more salespeople—it is about building a management infrastructure that prioritizes human performance as much as business performance. Companies that thrive in this transformation will be those that view the sales manager not only as a revenue driver, but as a steward of team culture, well-being, and sustainable performance.

Case Study: How Leading Companies Stay Ahead

Company: Nexora Technologies

Nexora Technologies, a global B2B software provider focused on enterprise data solutions, recognized early that their traditional sales compensation model was constraining growth. As their product offerings expanded into cloud-based subscriptions and usage-based pricing models, they needed a more agile and forward-thinking approach to incentivize their salesforce.

In response, Nexora implemented a hybrid compensation strategy. Sales reps were rewarded not only for closing new business but also for behaviours that drove long-term customer success—such as multi-product adoption, renewals, and usage milestones. The company also introduced quarterly bonuses tied to customer satisfaction scores and product engagement metrics, encouraging salespeople to think beyond the initial sale.

To embrace emerging technologies, Nexora piloted a generative AI tool integrated into their CRM. The AI assisted sales teams by generating personalized outreach emails, summarizing customer interactions, and identifying upsell opportunities. To drive adoption, Nexora added an "AI Proficiency Bonus," which rewarded sales reps who incorporated AI insights into their pipeline strategy and demonstrated measurable performance improvements.

Within six months, Nexora reported a 17% increase in average deal size and a 22% boost in customer retention rates. Sales cycle times shortened, and sales reps spent more time on high-impact conversations rather than administrative tasks. The shift also led to improved collaboration between sales and customer success teams, thanks to the shared performance metrics built into the new sales compensation model.

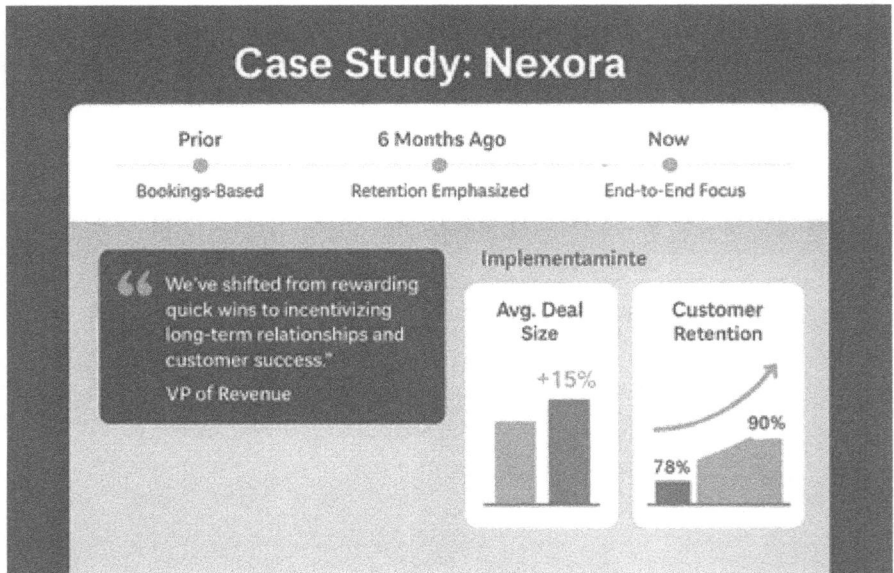

Case Study: Nexora

Prior	6 Months Ago	Now
Bookings-Based	Retention Emphasized	End-to-End Focus

Implementaminte

"We've shifted from rewarding quick wins to incentivizing long-term relationships and customer success."

VP of Revenue

Avg. Deal Size
+15%

Customer Retention
90%
78%

CONCLUSION

Sales compensation is no longer just a motivational lever—it is a strategic tool for aligning behaviour with business goals in a complex, fast-moving environment. The future of sales compensation is dynamic, data-driven, and deeply integrated with technology. By staying informed, flexible, and willing to experiment, companies can build compensation systems that not only reward performance but also shape it.

The future isn't something to wait for—it is something to build. Design for it now.

CHAPTER 11

Miscellaneous

Special Cases & Advanced Strategies in Sales Compensation

Not all sales compensation challenges fit neatly into a standard model. This chapter explores complex scenarios and edge cases to ensure your plan remains adaptable, fair, and effective in a variety of high-stakes situations.

> **How can companies structure compensation for unique cases like market expansions, hybrid roles, and multi-touch sales?**

Problem: Complexity Demands Customization Standard compensation frameworks often fall apart when confronted with edge cases. Consider the tension of managing hybrid roles where individuals sell, service, and consult—or the ambiguity of rewarding a deal closed by five people over six months across three departments. These situations demand nuance, and more importantly, intentionality. Without tailored strategies, companies risk misalignment, internal conflict, and missed targets.

The Result: Tailored Compensation Unlocks Control and Agility Companies that design flexible, scenario-specific compensation strategies build systems that adapt under pressure—without compromising performance or fairness.

Companies that design flexible, scenario-specific compensation strategies build systems that adapt under pressure—without compromising performance or fairness. The result is a resilient compensation model—one that supports growth across geographies, evolving sales motions, and organizational changes, while still maintaining fairness and motivation.

- ▶ Adapting to the complex realities of modern sales.
- ▶ Compensation for channel sales & partnerships – Designing incentives for indirect sales teams.
- ▶ International sales compensation – Navigating tax laws, currencies, and cultural differences.
- ▶ Handling draws & guarantees – When to use them, and how to phase them out.
- ▶ Multi-touch sales & team-based selling – Encouraging collaboration while maintaining accountability.
- ▶ Custom incentives for new product launches – Driving sales for innovative but unproven offerings.
- ▶ Managing compensation during mergers & acquisitions – Aligning sales teams without disruption.

Learnings: After reading this chapter, you will have a deep knowledge of how to address the most complex and atypical scenarios in sales compensation. You will be equipped to think strategically about how to adapt incentive structures to reflect real-world challenges, from cross-functional collaboration to international regulations and shifting product strategies. Most importantly, you will recognize the power of flexibility—not as a weakness in your compensation design, but as a strategic strength.

Not all sales compensation challenges follow conventional rules. As businesses scale, diversify, or restructure, compensation plans must rise to meet more complex demands. Whether you're entering new markets, navigating a merger, or launching a game-changing product, your ability to adapt your sales incentives determines not just performance, but cohesion, motivation, and long-term success.

Adapting to the Complex Realities of Modern Sales

Sales is no longer a linear, single-player game. Today's selling environments are multifaceted ecosystems involving multiple roles, evolving buyer journeys, and increasingly digital, cross-functional operations. As businesses scale or shift strategically, their compensation systems must evolve in tandem. Static compensation plans, even when well-designed initially, often fail under pressure when stretched across new geographies, product strategies, or organizational structures.

Modern sales strategies increasingly blur the traditional boundaries between roles, responsibilities, and revenue ownership. Inside and field reps work together in hybrid motions. Marketing contributes directly to revenue through demand generation and account-based initiatives. Customer success now drives retention and upsell, earning a spot on the revenue team. Sales engineers, solutions consultants, and even product managers may contribute meaningfully to complex deals. In such a reality, compensation becomes more than just pay—it becomes an orchestration tool that aligns behaviour with business outcomes across many champions.

To respond to this shift, compensation structures must be flexible, intelligent, and strategically segmented. Leaders must consider attribution models, regional differentiation, incentive layering, and timing with more granularity than ever before.

The sections that follow explore the most common—and most challenging—advanced compensation scenarios, and how to approach each with clarity and intention.

Compensation for Channel Sales & Partnerships – Designing Incentives for Indirect Sales Teams

Indirect sales motions—through resellers, distributors, affiliate partners, or strategic alliances—play a pivotal role in many companies' growth strategies. However, motivating partners pose–unique challenges, as these sellers aren't bound by the same cultural or operational levers as internal sales teams.

Unlike internal salespeople, channel partners typically juggle multiple products from different vendors. This means your incentive structure must not only be competitive but also simple, transparent, and compelling. Too many tiers, complex qualification rules, or limited visibility into rewards will dissuade partners from prioritizing your offering.

Effective channel compensation plans often include elements such as tiered commission structures, deal registration bonuses, co-marketing incentives, and milestone-based rewards (e.g., volume thresholds, new customer acquisition targets). Importantly, these plans must be supported by robust partner relationship management (PRM) systems to ensure accurate tracking and timely payouts.

To maintain alignment, companies should also consider non-monetary incentives—such as exclusive training, early access to new products, or co-branding opportunities—which can deepen loyalty and long-term engagement.

Compensation for Channel Sales & Partnerships
Designing Incentives for Indirect Sales Teams

Indirect Sales Incentives
- Tiered Commissions
- Deal Registration Bonuses
- Co-Marketing Incentives
- Milestone-Based Rewards

Alignment with Direct Sales

Shared Revenue Metrics

Partner Engagement

Milestones

International Sales Compensation – Navigating Tax Laws, Currencies, and Cultural Differences

Expanding into global markets brings both opportunity and complexity. Compensation strategies that work well domestically often require significant adjustment when applied internationally. Beyond differences in cost of living or taxation, cultural norms around pay structures, risk tolerance, and motivation can vary widely by region.

Currency exchange rates can create volatile earning experiences for salespeople if not properly managed. One solution is to denominate incentives in local currency and periodically adjust targets based on prevailing exchange rates. This ensures earnings feel stable and fair, without the sales rep being penalized by macroeconomic fluctuations beyond their control.

Tax regulations must also be navigated carefully. For instance, in some countries, variable compensation components are taxed differently from base salary or may trigger additional reporting burdens for the company. HR and legal teams must be involved in plan design to ensure compliance.

But perhaps the most nuanced challenge is cultural. In some markets, aggressive commission-based models are embraced; in others, they may be perceived as unstable or disrespectful. In regions where collectivism is more prominent, team-based or group incentives may be more motivating than individual bonuses. Sensitivity to these dynamics is essential for creating a globally consistent yet locally effective compensation strategy.

International Sales Compensation

Navigating Tax Laws, Currencies, and Cultural Differences

Currency Exchange
Manage fluctuations in earnings

Manage fluctuations in earnings

Tax Laws
Ensure compliance across regions

Cultural Differences
Adapt to local norms and preferences

Adapt to local norms and preferences

Handling Draws & Guarantees – When to Use Them, and How to Phase Them Out

Draws and guarantees are powerful tools in compensation strategy—especially when hiring new salespeople, launching into new markets, or dealing with unpredictable product adoption. But while these mechanisms can offer critical short-term stability, they must be structured carefully to avoid long-term dependency.

A **draw** is essentially an advance on future commissions. There are two types: *recoverable* (where the sales rep must pay back the draw if not earned through commission) and *non-recoverable* (where it functions more like a temporary base salary boost). Draws are most effective during onboarding, allowing new hires to ramp without the immediate pressure of full quota attainment.

Guarantees—fixed amounts of variable pay regardless of performance—are often used during territory transitions or major organizational changes. While they can stabilize morale, they can also disincentivize performance if maintained for too long or offered too generously.

The key to using these tools effectively lies in clear timelines and exit criteria. Draws should taper off as sales reps approach full productivity, and guarantees should come with transparent performance expectations. Communication is crucial: sales reps must understand when the additional support ends and what metrics they must meet to sustain their income through earned incentives.

Handling Draws & Guarantees

DRAWS
Advance on future
commissions

- Recoverable
- Non-recoverable

GUARANTEES
Fixed incentive
amounts

- Guaranteed pay
regardless of saes
performance

PHASING OUT SUPPORT

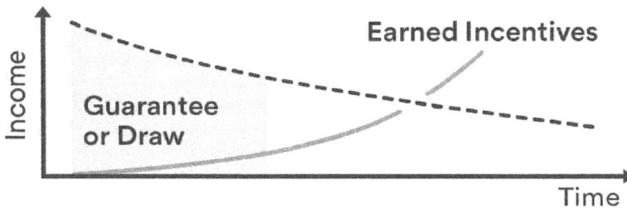

Earned Incentives

Income

Guarantee
or Draw

Time

Multi-Touch Sales & Team-Based Selling – Encouraging Collaboration While Maintaining Accountability

The rise of multi-touch sales processes—particularly in enterprise environments—means deals rarely belong to a single salesperson. Account executives, business development managers, solutions engineers, and customer success managers often collaborate across long, complex buying cycles. Compensation must evolve to reflect collective effort without losing the ability to hold individuals accountable for their unique contributions.

A strong multi-touch compensation plan does three things: it defines **contribution roles**, it allocates **credit fairly**, and it **preserves motivation** across all contributors. This might involve split commissions, role-based percentage payouts, or pooled incentive bonuses for team performance. However, it is vital to avoid diluting accountability; roles must be clearly defined, and attribution logic should be agreed upon upfront.

Some companies implement "deal teams" with shared quotas, where performance is judged collectively. Others use overlay roles—like technical specialists or customer success leads—who earn bonus multipliers or project-based bonuses based on successful participation in revenue-generating deals.

The balance is delicate. Incentives must foster trust and collaboration without making salespeople feel as though their personal efforts are lost in the crowd. Clear rules, transparent reporting, and ongoing calibration are key to success in this model.

MULTI–TOUCH SALES & TEAM-BASED SELLING

Encouraging Collaboration
While Maintaining Accountability

DEFINE CONTRIBUTION ROLES

ALLOCATE CREDIT FAIRLY

PRESERVE MOTIVATION

Split Commissions

Shared Quotas

Pooled Bonuses

Custom Incentives for New Product Launches – Driving Sales for Innovative but Unproven Offerings

When companies launch new products—especially in technology or SaaS—they often face a paradox: they need sales momentum to prove value, but few salespeople are eager to spend time on a product without a strong success record or proven commission potential In these moments, compensation becomes a strategic lever to spark internal adoption and accelerate market traction.

Custom incentives for new products can take many forms. Accelerators (higher commission rates for early deals), SPIFs (short-term bonuses for specific achievements), and milestone bounties (rewards for first sale, first renewal, or customer reference) are all effective when aligned with strategic goals. These incentives should be limited in duration, clearly communicated, and evaluated for ROI frequently.

One key is to protect sales reps from perceived risk. Salespeople are rational actors—they gravitate toward what is most likely to earn them predictable income. Offering transitional quotas, dual-crediting for new and core products, or quota relief tied to new-product activity can reduce friction and encourage experimentation.

Ultimately, product launch incentives should generate focused momentum—not permanently reshape the broader compensation architecture. When handled well, it can dramatically accelerate time-to-market success and build the product's early credibility with both sellers and buyers.

Managing Compensation During Mergers & Acquisitions – Aligning Sales Teams Without Disruption

Few events stress a compensation system like a merger or acquisition. Bringing together two (or more) sales teams—each with their own plans, cultures, and customer relationships—creates enormous complexity. Done poorly, compensation misalignment can lead to internal competition, salespeople attrition, and lost revenue. Done well, it becomes a unifying tool that signals fairness, vision, and opportunity.

During an M&A event, the first imperative is **continuity**—ensuring that sales teams feel financially secure and operationally stable during the transition. Sales professionals must not feel like their earnings are at immediate risk. This often means temporarily grandfathering existing plans while leadership analyses the new sales structure and builds a unified go-forward strategy.

Next comes **alignment**. Compensation plans must be reconciled to reflect the new business reality—roles may change, territories may be redrawn, and products may be cross-sold. This phase involves modelling scenarios, conducting fairness audits, and getting input from sales leaders to build credibility.

Finally, **integration**. A new plan must be introduced with empathy and clarity, ideally after a transition period that includes shadow quotas, optional opt-ins, or phased implementation. Transparency and communication are crucial, as compensation is emotional, and changes must be explained in terms of shared goals, opportunity, and future growth. As a rule: Whenever you are touching people's income, be very considerate.

Managing Compensation During Mergers & Acquisitions

Continuity

- Secure income
- Temporary plans
- Sales structure analysis

Alignment

- Plan reconciliation
- Scenario modelling
- Fairness audits

Integration

- New plan rollout
- Transition period
- Clear communication

This section is a reminder that sales compensation isn't a fixed formula—it is a living, evolving framework designed to reflect the complex realities of modern business. Whether expanding globally, launching new products, or navigating organizational change, success lies in the details—understanding the scenario, listening to the people it impacts, and designing with both data and empathy in mind.

CONCLUSION

Sales compensation is both a science and an art. It demands logic, structure, and fairness—but also empathy, foresight, and adaptability. While the earlier chapters of this book may have focused on the foundational principles, this final chapter highlights what separates good compensation design from great: The ability to handle any upcoming circumstances with clarity and confidence.

As you move forward in refining or rebuilding your compensation strategies, remember that the real world rarely fits the model perfectly. Plans will need to flex. Roles will evolve. Business will change. But if your compensation system is built with intention, intelligence, and room to grow, it can remain a driving force for motivation and performance—even in the most complex conditions.

In this final chapter, we have moved beyond foundational models to explore special cases and advanced strategies—those nuanced situations where generic approaches fall short and customization is critical.

This chapter—and this book—does not mark an endpoint, but the beginning of a new mindset. One where compensation is no longer reactive, but proactive. No longer rigid, but resilient. And above all, no longer just about pay—but about purpose.

APPENDIX

Practical Guides and Insights on Sales Compensation

1. Pay-Mix & Role Benchmarking

Pay-mix is the ratio of base salary to variable incentive that makes up a salesperson's On-Target Earnings (OTE). For example, a 70/30 pay-mix means that 70% of earnings are guaranteed salary, while 30% is tied to performance. Getting this balance right is critical, because it influences not only how salespeople are motivated, but also how attractive your roles appear in the talent market.

Role-based benchmarks in SaaS and B2B sales include:

- Sales Development Representatives (SDRs): 70/30 or 60/40. With a focus on meetings and bookings rather than closing deals, SDRs require more stability and less risk.
- Sales Engineers / Pre-Sales: 75/25 or 80/20. These technical experts influence deals but do not close them, so heavier base pay is standard.
- Account Managers (AMs): 70/30 or 80/20. Their role is retention, renewals, upsell and cross-sell, not net new.
- Enterprise or Strategic Account Executives: 50/50 or 60/40. Long, complex sales cycles justify a higher base to ensure stability.
- Business Development Managers (BDMs): 60/40. Performance-driven, with strong emphasis on new business creation.

Regional differences matter.

In North America, compensation is often more aggressive with a 50/50 mix common for hunters. In EMEA/APAC, stability is valued, so 60/40 is typical. In LATAM, practices vary depending on industry maturity.

A best practice: set pay-mix according to the influence of the role. Hunters who drive new logos should have aggressive variable pay. Farmers who manage renewals should have stability. Sales managers typically earn 10% less base pay ratio than their direct reports, ensuring alignment while recognizing leadership responsibility.

2. Commission Rates & Structures

Commission is the engine that fuels sales behaviour. While benchmarks vary, SaaS sales offer some useful guidelines:

▶ Standard Rates: 10% commission on Annual Contract Value (ACV) or Annual Recurring Revenue (ARR).
▶ Tiered Commissions: Higher percentages after quota attainment to encourage overperformance.
▶ Accelerators and Bonuses: Commonly used for multi-year deals or strategic wins. These amplify motivation when deals matter most.
▶ Quota-to-OTE Ratios: A 5:1 ratio is standard. A salesperson with $100K OTE typically carries a $500K annual quota. This ensures compensation is sustainable relative to revenue.
▶ Claw backs: To mitigate churn risk, many firms require repayment if customers cancel early.

A well-structured commission system balances fairness, competitiveness, and sustainability.

3. SPIF Template

Short-term incentives drive urgency.

SPIF (Sales Performance Incentive Fund):

▶ Provide small, targeted bonuses outside the core plan.

- ▸ Best used to launch new products, drive growth in new territories, boost high-margin sales, or clear old inventory.
- ▸ Keep them simple. Too many SPIFs at once dilute impact.

Simplified SPIF Template:

Program Name

Requester

Business Unit / Country

Business Issue (Provide a brief summary of the business issue the Bonus/SPIF is intended to address)

Program Details Purpose/Objectives
(*Describe the end results intended with this program*)

Program Duration Period

Program Eligibility (List the role eligibility for this program. Indicate all positions, including job codes and titles. Also cover whether any sales management (Execs, Managers, roll-up function) roles are eligible for the Bonus/SPIF)

Program Specifics (Provide an overview of the objectives and program specifics – how it works, payout amounts, criteria/frequency of payment etc. Include payment categories and payout amount if multiple levels are used. Describe specifically what must be done to earn the Bonus or SPIF (e.g. if focused on new business or a specific type of deal, what type and PLs eligible). List any applicable restrictions, caps etc. Are similar amounts paid to all individuals or is it a pool of money to be split among multiple individuals as determined per deal? Is there a minimum or maximum amount that can be paid to an individual participant? If yes, how much?)

Process Overview (Provide an overview of how the administration process will work. Is pre-registration required? Describe how the program is communicated, including individual goals/targets; how bonuses are validated, calculated and paid; and who is responsible for coordinating, pre-registration, claims, reporting sales data and payouts? List any special issues/approvals required. Describe how data will flow on targets, attainment, payments, etc.

Program Effectiveness Criteria (Define the metrics and targets for evaluating post program effectiveness. Who will be responsible for evaluating effectiveness?

Estimated ROI

Estimated Program Cost—by Cost Center

Maximum Program Cost

Percent of Total Participants

Eligibility/Winners Breakdown

Average Award

Percent of Variable Compensation

Maximum Award

Awards Breakdown

Funding Business Unit

SALES COMPENSATION PLAYBOOK \\

Program Mgr Contact

Region Sales VP Approver(s)

Region Sales VP Approver Date

Region Finance Approver(s)

Region Finance Approver Date

Mgmt Approver

Mgmt Approver Date

Region Mgr Approver(s)

Region Mgr Approver Date

Internal Notes

Status (Planning, open, active, closed)

Does this program require a policy exception?

Does this program keep the eligible population at 3 or fewer programs?

4. Plan Design Best Practices

Sales compensation plans succeed or fail based on design. Over-engineering leads to confusion. Under-designing leads to misalignment.

Best practices include:

1. Limit to 3 or fewer measurable components. Weighting should not drop below 20% for any element.
2. Focus on hard measures like revenue, quota attainment, or NRR. Soft measures (e.g., training, customer visits) belong in performance reviews, not compensation.
3. Keep the plan transparent and easy to explain. If sales reps can't calculate their earnings, motivation suffers.
4. Prioritize strategic objectives. Plans that try to cover everything achieve nothing.

Why plans fail:

▶ Poor quota setting
▶ Conflicting objectives
▶ Incomplete terms and conditions
▶ Lack of executive attention
▶ Weak communication

5. Forecasting & Quota Management

Forecasting is the foundation of business planning. Yet many sales leaders struggle with accuracy.

Why forecasts miss the mark:

▶ Over-optimism or sandbagging
▶ Lack of accountability for managers
▶ Counting unqualified opportunities
▶ Poor tool usage or data entry standards
▶ Misalignment with other departments

Fixing the problem:

- Hold managers accountable for forecast accuracy.
- Require evidence for forecasts.
- Compare forecast vs actual, then adjust training and expectations.
- Clean and validate pipeline data regularly.

Why accuracy matters:

Inaccurate forecasts mislead shareholders, distort financial planning, and erode credibility with investors. Accurate forecasts enable smarter decisions, realistic quota setting, and confidence across the organization.

Quota Management:

When a salesperson leaves mid-year, quota should be either redistributed across the team or absorbed by the manager. Incentives are typically prorated based on time served, though policies vary depending on whether the departure was voluntary or involuntary.

6. Roles & Responsibilities in Plan Design

Sales compensation is not a solo project. It requires cross-functional input.

Core contributors:

- Sales Compensation (project lead)
- Sales Management
- Finance
- HR
- Product Marketing
- Executive Leadership
- Legal and Sales Operations (where available)

Approval responsibilities:

Executives must go beyond rubber-stamping. Leaders should ask:

- Why is the plan changing?
- What exactly is different?

▸ Can we measure the outcomes?
▸ How is it being communicated?
▸ What is the cost vs revenue tradeoff?

Selling the sales compensation plan to your salesforce:

Your salespeople are the "buyers" of the plan. Communicate via Sales Kick-Off (SKO) and ongoing updates:

▸ Strategy highlights for the year
▸ Key changes year-over-year
▸ Examples of how earnings work
▸ Open channels for questions and feedback

7. Sales Methodologies & Changing Buyer Behaviour

Buyer behaviour has shifted. Customers do their homework before contacting vendors. This shortens cycles but raises expectations. Salespeople must meet buyers where they are.

Leading methodologies include:

▸ Solution Selling: Focuses on solving customer problems rather than pitching products.
▸ Miller-Heiman (Conceptual Selling): Aligns to the customer's perception of value.
▸ SPIN Selling: Uses structured questioning (Situation, Problem, Implication, Need-payoff).
▸ Challenger Sale: Teaches, tailors, and takes control of conversations.
▸ Sandler: Treats buyer and seller as equals, exiting quickly if misaligned.
▸ SNAP Selling: Emphasizes simplicity, alignment, and priorities.

Aligning sales compensation with selling methodology ensures salespeople are rewarded for behaviour consistent with strategy.

8. Negotiation & Leadership Skills

Sales is not just numbers; it is people. Successful professionals master key skills:

▶ Communication & Active Listening – avoid assumptions, ask open questions.
▶ Emotional Intelligence – manage stress, read signals, and respond empathetically.
▶ Creating Value – aim for win-win outcomes, not zero-sum bargaining.
▶ Preparation – understand the other party, their goals, and their constraints.
▶ Adaptability – negotiations shift quickly; flexibility is key.

Leaders must also manage toxic workplace personalities. Strategies include disconnecting emotionally, documenting behaviour, confronting respectfully, and escalating when needed.

9. Go-to-Market Planning & Strategy Integration

Sales compensation does not exist in isolation. It is a lever of go-to-market (GTM) strategy.

Key GTM elements:

▶ Market intelligence and segmentation
▶ Value proposition and pricing strategy
▶ Channel selection (direct vs partner)
▶ Compensation alignment with GTM priorities

Sales compensation plans must encourage sales behaviours that align with GTM — such as entering new markets, selling bundled solutions, or focusing on specific verticals.

10. Continuous Improvement & Review

Compensation plans are not "set and forget." Continuous evaluation ensures they stay effective.

Annual Review Practices:

▶ Conduct a Sales Compensation Excellence Forum mid-year to assess performance vs. plan.
▶ Evaluate alignment with company strategy.
▶ Identify gaps in behaviour or coverage.
▶ Adjust for market changes.
▶ Golden Rule: If you can't measure it, don't pay on it.

On-Time, Accurate (OTA) Payments:

Nothing erodes trust faster than delayed or incorrect payouts. Ensuring timely accuracy is as important as the plan design itself.

Closing Note

Sales compensation is one of the most powerful tools to drive revenue growth and shape sales force behaviour. When designed with clarity, focus, and alignment to strategy, it becomes a competitive advantage. This appendix has outlined practical frameworks, benchmarks, and tools that can guide leaders in building effective, motivating, and sustainable sales compensation programs.

www.ingramcontent.com/pod-product-compliance
Lightning Source LLC
Chambersburg PA
CBHW040856210326
41597CB00029B/4870